The
LEGENDS
of GOLF

By Melanie Hauser and Mike Purkey
Foreword by Arnold Palmer

The Legends of Golf: Twenty-Five Champions and A Lifetime of Competition
was developed and published by Tehabi Sports, an imprint of
Tehabi Books, Inc. Tehabi is the official book publishing
licensee of the PGA TOUR and has produced and published
many award-winning sports and other non-fiction books that
are recognized for their strong literary and visual content. Tehabi
works with national and international brands, corporations,
institutions, and nonprofit groups to identify, develop, and
implement comprehensive publishing programs. Tehabi Books
is located in San Diego, California. www.tehabi.com

President and Publisher: Chris Capen
Senior Vice President: Sam Lewis
Vice President and Creative Director: Karla Olson
Director, PGA TOUR Publishing Program: Marci Weinberg
Manager, Corporate Sales: Andrew Arias
Senior Art Director: Josie Delker
Designers: Kendra Triftshauser, Mark Santos, and Efrat Rafaeli
Editors: Terry Spohn and Betsy Holt
Editorial Assistant: Emily Henning
Copy Editor: Katie Franco
Proofreader: Virginia Marable

With special thanks to key individuals at the PGA TOUR for
their invaluable contributions in the creation of *The Legends of Golf*:
Donna Orender, Senior Vice President, Strategic Development;
Robert J. Combs, Senior Vice President, Public Relations and
Communications; Ward Clayton, Director, Editorial Services;
Jeff Adams, Director, Public Relations, Champions Tour; and
Maureen Feeley, Publications Assistant. And special thanks to
Bob Rosen and Jennifer Unter of RLR Associates.

Opening gallery images:
pp. 2–3: Jack Nicklaus and Arnold Palmer at the 1962 U.S. Open
pp. 4–5: Hale Irwin and Gary Player at the 1974 World
      Match Play
pp. 6–7: Lee Trevino and Chi Chi Rodriguez at the
      1998 GTE Suncoast Classic
pp. 8–9: Craig Stadler at the 2004 AT&T Pebble Beach Pro-Am

ISBN-13: 978-1-933208-04-6
ISBN-10: 1-933208-04-X

Library of Congress Cataloging-in-Publication Data

Hauser, Melanie.
  The legends of golf : twenty-five champions and a lifetime of
competition / by Melanie Hauser and Mike Purkey.
     p. cm.
  ISBN 1-933208-04-X (hardcover : alk. paper)
  1. Golf--Tournaments--United States. 2. Golfers--United States--
Anecdotes. 3. Champions Tour (Organization) I. Title.
  GV970.H38 2005
  796.352'66--dc22
                                                    2004031006

Tehabi Books offers special discounts for bulk purchases of *The
Legends of Golf*. Copies may be used for corporate hospitality, sales
promotions, and/or premium items. Specific needs can be met
with customized covers, letter inserts, single-copy mailing cartons
with a corporate imprint, and the repurposing of materials into
new editions. For more information, contact Andrew Arias,
Corporate Sales Manager, Tehabi Books, 4920 Carroll Canyon
Road, Suite 200, San Diego, California 92121-3735; 1-800-243-7259.

In the United States, trade bookstores and other book retailers
may contact Publishers Group West for sales and distribution
information at 1-800-788-3123. Specialty golf retailers may contact
The Booklegger for sales and distribution information at
1-800-262-1556.

In Canada, *The Legends of Golf* is distributed by Georgetown
Publications, Inc., 34 Armstrong Avenue, Georgetown, ON
L7G 4R9 CANADA; 1-888-595-3008.

Printed in Verona, Italy, by Editoriale Bortolazzi-Stei.
Tehabi is proud to partner with EBS in the printing and binding
of this and other titles in the PGA TOUR Publishing Program.

10 9 8 7 6 5 4 3 2 1

CONTENTS

Arnold Palmer gives a thumbs-up to his loyal fans while playing in his 50th and final Masters in 2004.

Because of golf, I can't imagine a better life, having met the many wonderful people the game has placed in my path. I always look ahead, and I knew, 25 years ago, that the Champions Tour was looking ahead, too. From the start it was more than just a museum where golfers would go to be on display. It was, and continues to be, a place where some of the best golf on the planet is played. The Champions Tour has given rise to some great golf moments and closer relationships with the fans, and the men on this Tour have helped expand the boundaries of competitive play.

I feel very fortunate to have played in my early years on the Tour with men who shaped the game and laid the foundation for people like me to reap the benefits. I learned from them how to respect the game, and I'm also lucky enough to have had the opportunity to pass that on. The Champions Tour was just starting when I turned 50, and I was lucky there, too. It gave me a new place to keep playing the game I love, to keep competing at a high level, maybe give a little more back, in some small way, to the game and the people associated with it who have been so good to me.

The stories told in this book represent a larger truth about the game that has meant so much to those of us who get to play it for a living: When we work at it, the game endures; when we honor it, its values endure. The memories are still being made and passed on here. As I look ahead, I can see the Champions Tour as a vital arena for a lifelong sport and all the things it stands for, and I'm happy and grateful to be a part of that.

Arnold Palmer

The
LEGACY

"We were the best of friends and we loved
each other a great deal, but we would tell
each other, 'I want to beat you like a drum.'
Today [that spirit of competition] still exists.
Can you believe at our age it still exists?"

—GARY PLAYER

The popularity of golf, as illustrated at the legendary 1955 U.S. Open at the Olympic Club, laid the groundwork for the Champions Tour.

G olf, more than any other sport, is one of tradition and legacy. In the course of play, golfers from one generation share with the next the joy, honor, and respect for the game that they learned from the players who came before them. Tiger Woods, Phil Mickelson, Vijay Singh, and Ernie Els play with Arnold Palmer and Jack Nicklaus, who played with Sam Snead and Tommy Bolt, who played with Byron Nelson and Ben Hogan, who played with Gene Sarazen and Walter Hagen. Across time moments are shared, memories are made, and the legacy of great golf is passed on.

The champions profiled on these pages understand great golf. Together they own 532 PGA TOUR wins, including 86 major championships. With each other and their predecessors, they share the skill and competitive fire that has allowed them to achieve this awesome record. But that alone does not make them legendary. More than any other group in golf history, they compete—and therefore share their legacy—across generations. While nearly all the men featured here won on the PGA TOUR, each of them went on to nurture and mature his skills, ultimately redefining his career and extending the limits of competition on the Champions Tour.

No other professional sport gives champions the opportunity to play into their 50s, 60s, or even 70s. Most professional athletes watch their skills slip as they age, but in golf, the loss of skill is balanced by experience and a deeper understanding of the game. Created in 1979, the Champions Tour has kept golf's greats competing—and us

watching—at an age when the legendary golfers of previous eras, such as Ben Hogan and Harry Vardon, had long since given up the competitive game. Unlike any other sporting event, the Champions Tour gives golf fans the chance to witness the full evolution of a great golfer's skills.

Because of their lifetime commitment to world-class, competitive golf, these players become

Gene Sarazen starts the 1999 Masters, an honor he enjoyed with fellow legends Byron Nelson and Sam Snead.

like old friends. We first saw many of their faces in black and white, flashing across a television screen. We were captivated by the shots, the smiles, the crucial putts that turned careers from ordinary to legendary. We watched Sam Snead ride his flawless swing to a record number of PGA TOUR victories. We cheered as Peter Thomson collected a mantle full of Claret Jugs for his five British Open titles. We were enthralled by Arnold

Palmer's incredible 1960 season, in which he won eight times and birdied six of the first seven holes in the final round U.S. Open—a feat that would later become a classic Palmer charge. We were stunned by Tom Watson's dramatic and prescient chip shot into the cup to snatch the 1982 U.S. Open from Jack Nicklaus. And we never forgot that incredible rally by the 46-year-old Nicklaus in the final round of the 1986 Masters, when he birdied seven of the last ten holes, passed eight players on the leader board with a 30 over the final nine, and slipped into the green jacket for the sixth and final time.

The men profiled on these pages are here because of their contribution to golf, whether from performance, character, legacy, or a combination of all three. Each one is a legend in his own right. The Champions Tour affords these legends the opportunity to play with the younger professionals of today and to pass on the honor and respect for the game that they learned from those who came before them. These men, whose careers are intertwined with those of Byron Nelson, Walter Hagen, and Jimmy Demaret, carry golf's important stories forward, preserving the legacy of the sport and bringing new meaning to the history of the game. Gene Sarazen's double-eagle, for example, takes on special meaning when Byron Nelson recounts that he was over on the next fairway. Tom Watson, who learned at Nelson's knee, loves to talk about his mentor's marvelous streak of 11 straight wins.

Byron Nelson (right) and Sam Snead (middle) fought some epic battles on the PGA TOUR in the 1940s.

Jack Nicklaus (left) and Arnold Palmer, share a light moment with Greg Norman (right) at the 1990 Masters.

You won't find profiles here of Demaret, Nelson, Hogan, or Hagen, though. Their legendary careers ended long ago. But some of those profiled here went head-to-head with the men who drove cross-country for the chance to play in the 1940s and 1950s; some got the chance to play with Bobby Jones and Gene Sarazen in their prime.

What if senior golf had been here from the beginning? Would Hogan, Hagen, and Nelson have played on? Would those legends have been able to play into their 70s like Sam Snead and Arnold Palmer did? We'll never know.

What we do know is that the Champions Tour has made the sport seem ageless. It offers the chance for golf's greats to explore the mistakes of the past and turn them into strengths—giving them the opportunity to extend their legacy just a bit further. It also allows both players and fans to see the whole spectrum of the sport. We think back to the early days of Tom Watson, Craig Stadler, or Arnold Palmer. We recall Jackie Burke Jr., Jimmy Demaret, Byron Nelson, and Ben Hogan, while looking ahead to Tom Kite, Ben Crenshaw, and Justin Leonard. Tiger Woods, Sergio Garcia, and Phil Mickelson are decades away from playing the Champions Tour, but they are already part of the continuum that makes golf an ageless game.

Golf isn't a game of secrets. It's a game that's shared. It's about Gene Sarazen inventing the sand wedge, Byron Nelson teaching Tom Watson, and Arnold Palmer putting his arm around a young amateur named Tiger Woods and explaining how to read those seemingly incomprehensible greens. It's about Jack Nicklaus taking a lesson from Greg Norman, and Hale Irwin and Tom Watson challenging the up-and-comers to try to break their records. It's about old faces and new ones—the legacies and lessons that are passed on and preserved through the great game of golf.

The old guard—Lee Trevino (left) and Jack Nicklaus—shared the stage with up-and-comers like Sergio Garcia (right) at the 2002 Battle of the Bighorn.

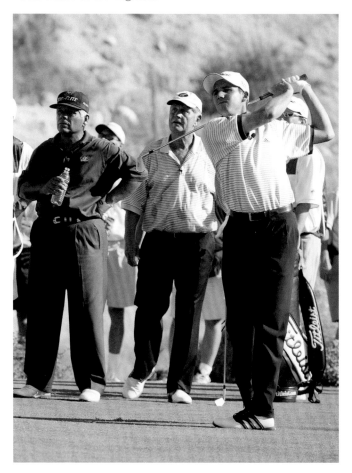

The Champions Tour draws crowds from all age groups and all walks of life, as seen at the 2004 JELD-WEN Tradition.

2

Chapter Two

The
LEGENDS

"I was a better player at 50
than I was at 30."

—SAM SNEAD

George Archer, wearing the coveted
green jacket, mingles with the
gallery after his phenomenal—
and unexpected—win at the
1969 Masters.

George Archer

George Archer always stood out from the crowd. That happens when you're a half-inch shy of six feet six, but that's not the only reason. He was always blunt, never afraid to say what he thought. And while he stood out physically in the PGA TOUR crowd, his game also set him apart, helping him reach the pinnacle when he won the 1969 Masters, forever securing him a place in that legendary event.

Archer won that Masters in a star-studded field, many of whom were on the leader board. He beat Billy Casper, one of the greatest players of all time, by one shot when Casper shot a final-round 74. Also in close pursuit were George Knudson, one of the greatest ball-strikers of all time; the mercurial Tom Weiskopf; and Charles Coody, who would win the green jacket in 1971.

While Archer had an outstanding career on the TOUR, winning a total of 12 tournaments, his star really began to shine as a senior. In 1989, two weeks after he turned 50, he won his debut on the Champions Tour at the Gatlin Brothers Southwest Classic in a playoff over Orville Moody and Jimmy Powell. Archer became the sixth player to win in his first start and was the youngest to have done so at the time.

Over the next three years, he was a dominant force. He won four times in his first full year on the Tour. In 1991, he was second to Mike Hill on the money list and shared Player of the Year honors with Hill. Archer won three times that year, including the GTE North Classic with a then-record score of 199. Most impressive were his 18 top five finishes.

He finished second on the money list in 1992 for the second consecutive year, and won three more events, including his third straight Northville Long Island Classic victory.

George Archer

Finished among the PGA TOUR's top five money-winners in 1968, 1971, and 1972

* * *

Turned professional: 1964

* * *

PGA TOUR victories: 12, including one Masters

* * *

Champions Tour victories: 19

Archer's swing was not the most classic. But his short game was superb, and he was considered one of the game's all-time great putters. At one time, he held the PGA TOUR record for fewest putts in a 72-hole tournament, when he needed only 95 at the 1980 Sea Pines Heritage Classic. That's just over 27 putts per round, a remarkable feat.

Over the years, the wear and tear on his body—he had three surgeries while playing on the PGA TOUR—took its toll and he thought about quitting. Instead, he had a knee and hip replaced and, at age 60, with those new body parts, he won the 2000 MasterCard Championship.

"My knee's only a few months old, my back is only 17, and I recently got a new hip," he said. "I might be too young now."

Stand out? Archer did. But as blunt as he was, he was also quotable. One time, when asked about retiring, he said, "Baseball players quit playing, and they take up golf. Basketball players quit, take up golf. Football players quit, take up golf. What are we supposed to take up when we quit?"

Archer won 19 times on the Champions Tour, including the 1995 Toshiba Senior Classic.

Renowned for his excellent short game, Archer tackles a bunker shot during the 1999 Senior Tour Championship.

Miller Barber walks triumphantly to the 12th hole at the Champions Golf Club after sinking a 25-foot putt in the first round of the 1969 U.S. Open.

Miller Barber

He's always been the mysterious Mr. X. Miller Barber was the man behind the dark glasses before dark glasses were cool, the man no one could find once he had left the course. "Back in my single days I dated a lot of different girls," Barber explained. "And when the James Bond movies came out, they called me 007. Then Mystery Man. Then X. It stuck with me all the way through. It gave me an identity."

Mr. X, who has a swing that was once described as resembling the motions of a taffy-pulling machine, won his first PGA TOUR event in 1964, went on to win 10 more times, and finally settled down and got married at age 39.

Barber was a solid, if unspectacular player on the PGA TOUR. That loopy swing was far from textbook, but it did produce results. He always seemed to hit the ball right on the nose. His list of victories might not seem impressive, but his 11 TOUR wins during the time when Jack Nicklaus, Arnold Palmer, Lee Trevino, and Tom Watson were all in their heyday were well earned.

Though his swing was far from classic, Barber was one of the purest ball-strikers in the game.

Miller Barber

Only winner of three
U.S. Senior Opens

* * *

Turned professional: 1958

* * *

PGA TOUR victories: 11

* * *

Champions Tour victories: 24,
including three U.S. Senior
Opens, one Senior PGA
Championship, and one Ford
Senior Players Championship

When Barber turned 50 in 1981, he committed himself to what was then called the Senior PGA Tour, eventually serving on the players' advisory board. He was one of the stars of the early days of the Tour, winning three times in six starts in 1981, when there were only seven tournaments on the schedule. He won the Senior PGA Championship in Palm Beach Gardens, Florida, by two strokes over Arnold Palmer, and finished in the top 10 in each of the events he entered.

In 1982, the third year of the Tour and the second for which Barber was eligible, he won three times, including the U.S. Senior Open. He led the money list those first two years, and in 1983, he won the inaugural Senior Tournament Players Championship—now the Ford Senior Players Championship—by one shot over Gene Littler.

Among his 24 senior victories, he won two more U.S. Senior Opens, in 1984 and 1985. He finished second on the money list to close friend Don January both those years. By then, the Senior PGA Tour was in full swing.

Happiness to Barber has always been a hotel room key in his pocket and a course to play. And, after 46 years on the two tours, he isn't slowing down. "The golf tours have been so rewarding to me," Barber said. "They've given me things that I could never have had in any other job."

Barber owns 24 Champions Tour victories, including three U.S. Senior Opens.

Tommy Bolt was legendary for his club-throwing prowess, although he always said those feats were exaggerated.

Tommy Bolt

Tommy Bolt swore he never threw more than five or six clubs in his life. But to hear people tell it, he was the orneriest man in the game. "Terrible Tommy." "Thunderbolt." He said it was heat and humidity that made his grips so slick the club would just fly right out of his hands—but never as often as those old sports writers said. "I never was mad at anyone, never killed anyone," Bolt said in 1980. "But you'd think I'd slaughtered 'em and buried 'em beside the fairway. John Dillinger couldn't kill as many people as I did. Shoot, ol' Bobby Jones threw more clubs than I ever saw, but he became immortal."

Bolt thundered his way into the World Golf Hall of Fame with 11 PGA TOUR wins, including the 1958 U.S. Open title at Southern Hills. Some called it the "Blast Furnace Open," owing to the fact that temperatures pushed the 100-degree mark all week. Combine that with the slick Southern Hills greens, and scores skyrocketed.

Gene Sarazen shot an 84 and Sam Snead shot rounds of 75-80 and missed the cut. But Bolt claimed to be serene. In fact, he carried a card in his pocket with the Serenity Prayer printed on it: "God grant me the serenity to accept the things I cannot change, the courage to change the things I can, and the wisdom to know the difference."

"I was happy," he said. "Nothing could make me mad. I was the complete master of my emotions that week. I birdied the first hole and I looked back toward the clubhouse and I thought, 'Well, I wonder who's going to finish second,'" remembered Bolt, who never relin-

Bolt was nicknamed "Terrible Tommy" and "Thunderbolt," names earned because of his tendency to do things like kick his golf ball after missing a putt.

quished the lead. He never shot a round higher than 72 and finished four shots ahead of 22-year-old Gary Player.

Bolt says that his game turned around when he came under the special tutelage of the great Ben Hogan, who cured his vicious hook. At the Memphis Open, Bolt had a chance to show off his stuff to his mentor. Bolt was in a three-way play-off with Hogan and Gene Littler and sealed the deal with a 2-iron at the par-3 17th that never left the flag.

"When Ben said, 'Nice shot!' it was like a double clap of thunder to me," said Bolt. "It was the only thing he had said to me all day. That's enough psychological therapy to last a golfer six months."

Bolt was one of the pioneers of the modern Champions Tour. He won the 1969 PGA Seniors Championship and 11 other world-wide senior titles. He was a star of the 1979 Liberty Mutual Legends of Golf when he and Art Wall went birdie-for-birdie with Roberto De Vicenzo and Julius Boros in a six-hole playoff until their opponents won with a sixth straight birdie.

"Roberto and I really enjoyed the playoff," Bolt said before the 25th anniversary of the tourna-ment. "We'd make a putt and point a finger at the other one. That's the first time I ever lost and enjoyed it. We showed that the old guys could still play."

1958 U.S. Open: Bolt's crowning achievement was winning at Southern Hills in Oklahoma.

Tommy Bolt

One of the founding members of the Champions Tour

* * *

Won the 1980 Liberty Mutual Legends of Golf with Art Wall

* * *

Turned professional: 1951

* * *

PGA TOUR victories: 15, including one U.S. Open

* * *

Inducted into the World Golf Hall of Fame in 2002

WORLD GOLF
HALL
of
FAME

 "You should always throw a club ahead of you so that you don't have to walk any extra distance to get it."

—TOMMY BOLT

The following year Bolt teamed up with Wall again at Liberty Mutual Legends of Golf to win his final tournament at age 62.

Bolt's favorite tale of thunder, by the way, is the one legendary writer Dan Jenkins dubbed No. 1,032 in a line of 5,000 or so. In this one, a local paper turned 39-year-old Bolt into 49-year-old Bolt. The writer apologized for the typographical error. "Typographical error my #$%," Bolt said. "It was a perfect four and a perfect nine."

One year at The Masters, Bolt tossed or broke so many clubs that, when faced with a 125-yard shot into the final green, Bolt asked his caddie for his 8-iron and got a 2-iron. It was the only club left.

Legendary explosions aside, Bolt was one of the great shotmakers in the game, and when his putter was hot, he was better than almost anyone else. And his temper never did run as hot as everyone thinks it did. At least that's what he says.

Bolt was a central figure in both the 1979 and 1980 Liberty Mutual Legends of Golf tournaments.

Bolt chats with Frank Sinatra, who personally listed Bolt's leading score at the 1963 Frank Sinatra Invitational, a PGA TOUR event that the famous crooner sponsored.

Julius Boros is all smiles after winning the 1963 U.S. Open at The Country Club in Brookline, Massachusetts.

Julius Boros

He didn't know it at the time, but Julius Boros was one of the central players in an all-star cast that would blossom into the Champions Tour. He teamed with Roberto De Vicenzo to win the now-famous 1979 Liberty Mutual Legends of Golf playoff over Tommy Bolt and Art Wall, a captivating event that brought senior golf into the consciousness of mainstream golf. That dramatic six-hole playoff convinced many people—including the players themselves—that senior golf was viable from the standpoint of fans, sponsors, and television.

Boros was one of the original six that formed the nucleus of the Tour that began in 1980. Although he was 60 at the time and never won on the fledgling Tour, Boros lent his legendary star power at a time when the Tour needed it most—in the beginning. His participation brought credibility to the new venture.

Boros had been an accountant when, at age 30, he decided to become a professional golfer. His debut was at the 1950 U.S. Open at Merion where he tied for 10th. Two years later, he would be crowned U.S. Open champion at Northwood Country Club in Dallas, the first of his three major championships. He also won the World Championship that year, which paid a first place prize of $50,000, an unheard of sum at that time.

Boros had one of his biggest years in 1963, winning the Colonial National Invitation for the second time, the Buick Open, and the U.S. Open title—all at the age of 43.

Boros emerged victorious at the 1963 U.S. Open by surviving a three-way playoff with Arnold Palmer (center) and Jacky Cupit.

"By the time you get to your ball, if you don't know what to do with it, try another sport." —JULIUS BOROS

Boros's mantra was "swing easy, hit hard," as evidenced by his flowing, rhythmic swing.

At the 1963 U.S. Open, Boros survived vicious winds that buffeted The Country Club in Brookline, Massachusetts, and the onslaught of Arnold Palmer. The winds were so formidable that defending champion Jack Nicklaus missed the cut, Sam Snead shot 83, and Tommy Aaron posted a 91.

Jacky Cupit led Palmer by one and Boros by three, despite a 5-over 76 in the third round. In fact, the whole championship had been a war of attrition, producing the highest Open scores in years. Cupit managed rounds of 70-72-76—218, 5-over par on the par-71 layout. Palmer shot 77 in the third round to go with rounds of 73-69 and come in at 219 after 54 holes. Boros posted rounds of 71-74-76—221, 8-over par.

The entire final day had the aura of a prize-fight, with the competitors slugging it out against the elements, the difficult course, and each other. The affair was essentially in deadlock at the 17th, where Cupit made a double bogey and Palmer three-putted for a bogey, throwing the championship into a three-way tie, at 9-over-par 293.

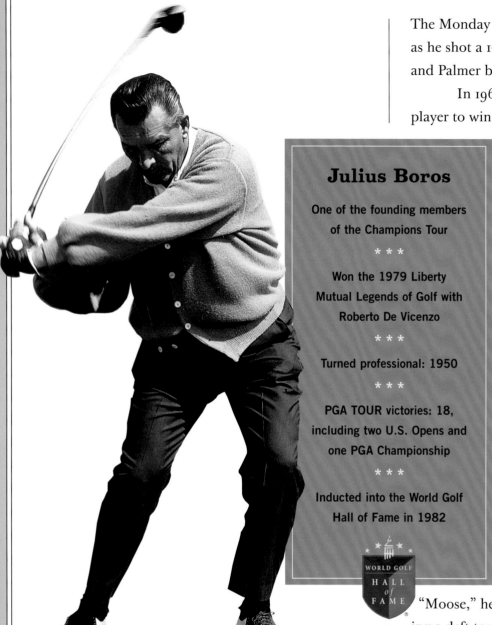

The Monday playoff belonged exclusively to Boros, as he shot a 1-under-par 70 to beat Cupit by three and Palmer by six.

In 1968, at age 48, he became the oldest player to win a major championship, coming away with the PGA Championship title at Pecan Valley Country Club in San Antonio. In all, Boros had 18 PGA TOUR wins and was considered one of the most successful players of his time.

He was a big man, at six feet and more than 200 pounds, but he was not an imposing figure. In fact, he lumbered along with a leisurely gait and was often seen with a blade of grass or a toothpick dangling from his lip. His watchwords were, "Swing easy, hit hard," and his action certainly lived up to the billing. He swung easily and fluidly, but got the clubhead through the hitting zone with surprising speed. And, although a big man with the nickname "Moose," he was anything but, capable of displaying a deft touch around the greens.

Boros was PGA Player of the Year in 1952 and 1963, played on four Ryder Cup teams, and was elected into the World Golf Hall of Fame in 1982. He died in 1994, at age 74, leaving a lasting legacy to the Tour he helped found.

Julius Boros

One of the founding members
of the Champions Tour

* * *

Won the 1979 Liberty
Mutual Legends of Golf with
Roberto De Vicenzo

* * *

Turned professional: 1950

* * *

PGA TOUR victories: 18,
including two U.S. Opens and
one PGA Championship

* * *

Inducted into the World Golf
Hall of Fame in 1982

WORLD GOLF
HALL
of
FAME

Along with partner Roberto De Vicenzo, Boros won the now-famous 1979 Liberty Mutual Legends of Golf, beating Tommy Bolt and Art Wall in a six-hole playoff.

At age 48, Boros became the oldest player to ever win a major championship, capturing the PGA Championship in 1968 at Pecan Valley Country Club in San Antonio—his third career major.

Billy Casper, one of the game's greatest putters, studies his putt at the 1970 Masters on the 18th green at Augusta National. He eventually won in a playoff over Gene Littler.

Billy Casper

He is perhaps the most underrated, underappreciated superstar of the modern era. In the 1960s, golf was dominated by the "Big Three"—Arnold Palmer, Jack Nicklaus, and Gary Player. But there was a fourth: Billy Casper.

Very quietly and unassumingly, Casper amassed 51 victories on the PGA TOUR, the sixth highest win total in history behind Sam Snead, Jack Nicklaus, Ben Hogan, Arnold Palmer, and Byron Nelson— some pretty heady company. But if you're younger than 40, you might have never heard of Casper.

His greatest triumph came at the expense of Palmer in the 1966 U.S. Open at the Olympic Club in San Francisco. Casper shot 69-68 in the first two rounds to tie Palmer, who carded 71-66, for the lead. They were paired together for the third round when Palmer took a three-shot lead with an even-par 70, while Casper slipped with a 73.

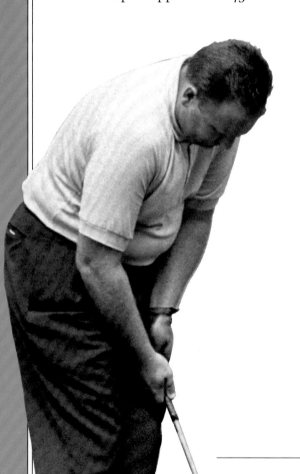

Casper was modest about his putting skills. "Oh, I used to make 'em once in a while," he said.

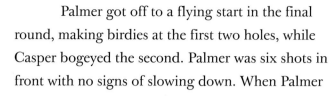

Billy Casper

Won at least one tournament in 16 consecutive years, second only to Nicklaus and Palmer

* * *

PGA TOUR victories: 51, including two U.S. Opens and one Masters

* * *

Champions Tour victories: Nine, including one Ford Senior Players Championship and one U.S. Senior Open

* * *

Turned professional: 1954

* * *

Last year competing: 2001

* * *

Inducted into the World Golf Hall of Fame in 1978

Palmer got off to a flying start in the final round, making birdies at the first two holes, while Casper bogeyed the second. Palmer was six shots in front with no signs of slowing down. When Palmer carded an outward nine of 32, he led by seven with nine holes to play. At the time, Palmer was 6-under par and chasing Ben Hogan's U.S. Open record (at the time) of 276.

He and Casper stood at the 10th tee and Casper said to Palmer, "I'm really going to have to go to get second."

Palmer replied, "Don't worry, Bill. You'll get second."

With four holes to play, Palmer led by five. But Casper birdied 15 while Palmer bogeyed to cut the lead to three. At the 16th, Palmer stumbled to another bogey while Casper made a second straight birdie. Now, the lead was one. At the 17th, both missed the green, but Casper pitched his second shot to four feet. He made his par while Palmer missed, and they were tied. A couple of pars at the last hole assured a Monday playoff.

Palmer bolted out of the gate in the playoff and led by two at the turn. But at the 13th, Casper made a 50-foot putt to go one up. Palmer faltered down the stretch and Casper wound up winning the playoff with a 69 to Palmer's 73.

Arnold Palmer congratulates Casper (right) after the 1966 U.S. Open. Casper won over Palmer in a playoff by sinking his final putt on the 18th green at the Olympic Club in San Francisco.

Casper was known as one of the best putters the game had ever seen. In his victory at the 1959 U.S. Open at Winged Foot, Casper led an impressive leader board that featured future Hall of Famers Palmer, Snead, and Hogan. It was Casper's formidable putter that brought home the Open trophy for him. He needed only 114 putts for the four rounds, including just 27 in the third round and 28 in the fourth. He one-putted 31 times in 72 holes and three-putted only once.

Casper, winner of the inaugural 1958 Buick Open, shares a moment with Tiger Woods at the 2003 event.

Hogan was said to have told Casper, "If you couldn't putt, you'd be selling hot dogs at the turn."

When Casper won the 1970 Masters, it was also in a playoff. He led Gene Littler by one going into Sunday's final round. Littler shot 2-under 70 against Casper's 71 to force a Monday playoff. Casper putted his way to a 69 in the playoff to Littler's 73 to win the green jacket.

Virtually no one remembers that Casper had a very good chance to win the 1968 British Open at Carnoustie, perhaps the most difficult course in the world when the wind blows. Casper shot a 4-under 68 to lead by four over Bob Charles after 36 holes. He retained a one-shot lead after 54 holes, despite a 2-over 74, but shot a windblown 78 on the final day, and Gary Player won the championship.

From 1956 to 1971, Casper won at least one tournament each year. Twenty-nine of those wins came between 1962 and 1969. No one besides Nicklaus had won as often. Casper was the PGA TOUR Player of the Year in 1966 and 1970 and would have won the award more often had it not been for Nicklaus.

He played on eight Ryder Cup teams and was captain in 1979. He won the Vardon Trophy for lowest scoring average in 1960, 1963, 1965, 1966, and 1968. He was inducted into the World Golf Hall of Fame in 1982.

After he turned 50 in 1981, he played enough to win nine tournaments in eight seasons, including two majors—the 1983 U.S. Senior Open and the 1988 Senior Tournament Players Championship—all the while doing what he always did: putt the lights out.

Whether he was blasting out of the sand or driving off the tee, Billy Casper never had classic form until he got the ball onto the green. There he was unmatched.

Bob Charles won the Picadilly World Match Play title in 1969 at Wentworth Golf Club in England. It was one of 24 international victories.

Bob Charles

Until Phil Mickelson and Mike Weir came along, the best left-hander in the game for decades was New Zealand native Bob Charles. Charles grew up wanting to a be a rugby star until an injury cut short that dream.

More than five decades later, the 69-year-old is still playing full time on the Champions Tour. Charles is one of those players who became much more of a legend as a senior than he did playing the PGA TOUR. But he exemplified the quintessential Champions Tour success story: Be a relatively straight hitter, keep the ball in play, be a great putter, and you'll guarantee victory.

Charles always was one of the great putters in golf. His skill at putting is precisely the reason he won the 1963 British Open at Royal Lytham and St. Annes. In the third round, he shot a 5-under par 66 that gave him a one-shot lead over five-time champion Peter Thomson and put him two shots ahead of Jack Nicklaus and Phil Rodgers. On the way to his 66, he made several impressive putts for birdies and pars.

Rodgers made up the two shots in the final round to force what was to be the last 36-hole playoff in British Open history. But Charles

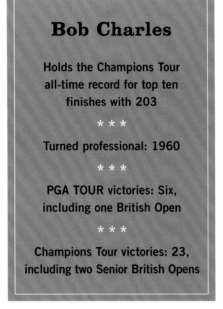

Bob Charles

Holds the Champions Tour all-time record for top ten finishes with 203

* * *

Turned professional: 1960

* * *

PGA TOUR victories: Six, including one British Open

* * *

Champions Tour victories: 23, including two Senior British Opens

Even at age 68, Charles still competes in international events, this time at the 2004 New Zealand Open in his native country.

continued his hot putting to shoot 2-under 140 in the playoff to defeat Rodgers by eight strokes.

Charles won only five other events, but he remained a solid player on the PGA TOUR. In the meantime, he won 24 international events, including the prestigious Picadilly World Match Play in 1969.

After turning 50, Charles blossomed in America. In 1987, his second year on the Champions Tour, he won three times. In 1988 and 1989, he won five events both years, was the leading money winner each year, and was twice named Player of the Year. He was a consistent winner in subsequent years, taking 23 titles in all. In 1993 he made another run at the money title but finished second to Dave Stockton.

He played golf left-handed and did everything else right-handed. A quiet man, he never showed much emotion on the course. His trademark celebration was a tap on the bill of his visor. When asked about his lack of emotion, he likened himself to tennis great Bjorn Borg, who also went about his championship business without a smile on his face.

Of his longevity in the game he said, "It's the fascination of the game and how you can never master it. It's the one, two, three, or four good shots that I happen to hit in a round that keep bringing me back. Of course I'd rather forget the one, two, three, or four bad ones."

Hoisting the Claret Jug at the 1963 British Open, Charles celebrates his crowning achievement which finally came after defeating Phil Rodgers in a 36-hole playoff.

Jim Colbert is one of the most prolific players in Champions Tour history, having won 20 times. He also shares with Chi Chi Rodriguez the Tour's all-time best birdie streak at eight.

Jim Colbert

A bad back knocked the man with the flipped-up collar and bucket hat off the PGA TOUR. It also gave him a second chance. Jim Colbert spent three years resting his chronic back, analyzing other players' games for ESPN, and learning a bit about himself in the process. And just before turning 50, he sold his golf course company and joined the Champions Tour.

Colbert firmly believes that his work in the television booth helped him realize things about the game that he couldn't see otherwise. Colbert took that knowledge and applied it well. While he was only a modest success as a PGA

TOUR player, he has made himself one of the most successful seniors in the game.

His 20 victories on the Champions Tour put him in the top 10 in all-time victories, ahead of more highly regarded legends of the game like Gary Player, Dave Stockton, Raymond Floyd, Arnold Palmer, and Jack Nicklaus. Colbert's newfound success has placed him among the top five in career Champions Tour earnings.

He won eight times on the PGA TOUR from 1969 to 1983, when the likes of Jack Nicklaus, Lee Trevino, and Tom Watson were in their prime and dominating the leader boards each week. Colbert's best year was 1983 when he won the prestigious Colonial National Invitation and the Texas Open.

Once he turned 50, though, his career took off. From his rookie year in 1991 through 1996, he won at least twice each year, and proved himself a force to be reckoned with. He won three times—the first in his hometown of Kansas City—in his first six months as a senior. He finished second five times, made nearly $900,000, and was Rookie of the Year. Not bad for a man who had been hurting so badly he played the 1987 U.S. Open while taking pain medication and with an electronic device on his lower back.

Colbert won four times during the next two seasons and twice more in 1994. He discovered

Jim Colbert

Youngest player ever to shoot his age in a Champions Tour major

* * *

Turned professional: 1965

* * *

PGA TOUR victories: Eight

* * *

Champions Tour victories: 20, including one Ford Senior Players Championship

the power of magnets and wore them on his back to reduce pain. By the time 1995 rolled around, he was ready to hit the fast-forward button on his career. He won four times in 1995 and won five events the following year, leading the money list both seasons.

He underwent surgery for prostate cancer in 1997, but came back to win The Transamerica in 1998 and added the 2001 SBC Senior Classic for his 20th win. He has since joined fellow survivors like Ray Floyd and Arnold Palmer in the battle to educate people about prostate cancer.

Colbert has endured much to become a Champions Tour success. But his place in senior history is secure.

Colbert won the 1983 Colonial National Invitation, one of the most prestigious events on the PGA TOUR.

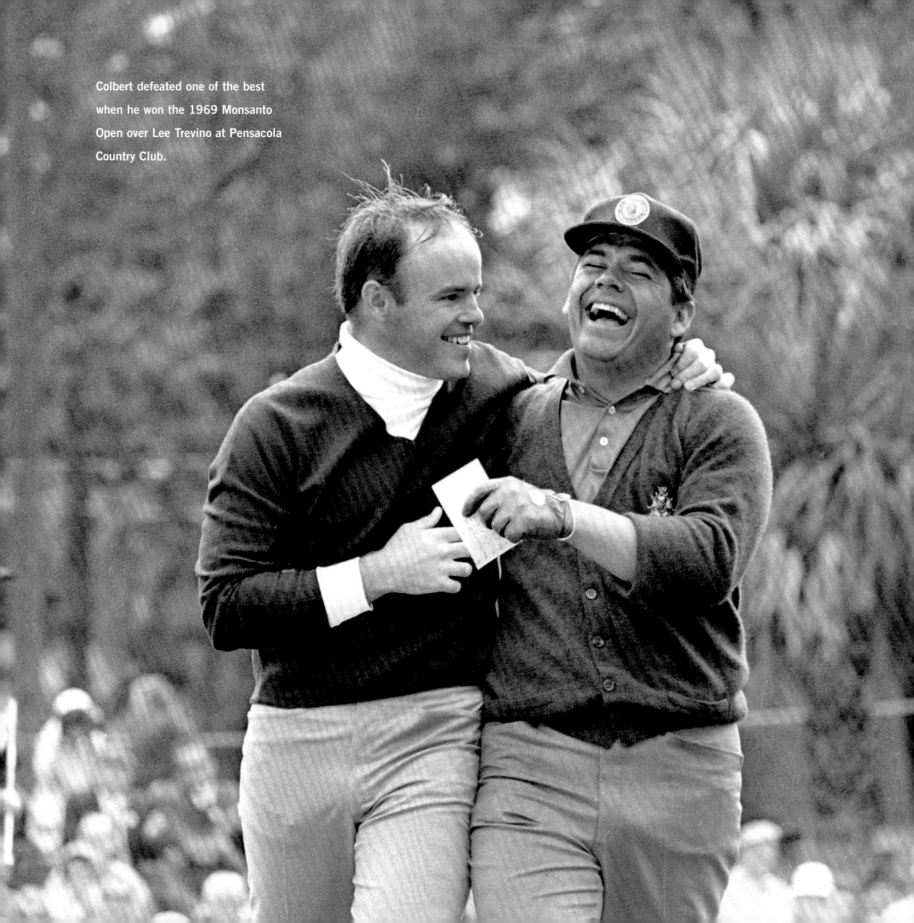

Colbert defeated one of the best when he won the 1969 Monsanto Open over Lee Trevino at Pensacola Country Club.

One of the inspirational success stories on the Champions Tour, Allen Doyle turned a stellar amateur career into a lucrative professional career.

Allen Doyle

Even when Allen Doyle was working in a textile mill, he spent his spare time on the golf course. And when his boss told him he couldn't arrange his vacation and days off to play in amateur events, Doyle bought a driving range in LaGrange, Georgia, where he was content to tell stories and rent range balls, all while teeing it up in amateur events against kids named Tiger Woods and Phil Mickelson.

Doyle was one of the top amateurs in the country for a number of years. He dominated Georgia amateur golf, winning the state amateur in back-to-back years on two separate occasions almost ten years apart. In 1994, he won the prestigious Porter Cup, the Sunnehanna Amateur, the Cardinal Amateur, the Dogwood Amateur, and the Rice Planters Invitational. Along the way, he was named to three Walker Cup teams.

The next year, at age 46, he turned pro and played the 1995 season on what was then the Nike Tour. Amazingly, he won three times, including the Nike Tour Championship at the end of the season. Those victories entitled him to go to the next level where, at age 47, he became the oldest player ever to qualify for the PGA TOUR. Although he never won on TOUR, he played well enough to retain his card until he turned 50.

"I sat down at the end of [1994] and I couldn't do any more as an amateur," he said.

"So what did I need to do to keep working hard until I was 50? That was to turn pro. I felt like if I worked hard in my late 40s, that would provide me with my best shot out here."

Three years later, he was walking up the 18th

Allen Doyle

First player to triumph on both the Nationwide Tour and the Champions Tour

* * *

Nationwide Tour victories: Three

* * *

Earned 19 amateur victories from 1978 to 1994

* * *

Turned professional: 1995

* * *

Champions Tour victories: Nine, including one Senior PGA Championship and one Ford Senior Players Championship

fairway at the Champions Tour Qualifying Tournament with Bruce Fleisher, for whom he had once caddied, and they were both going to qualify—Doyle as medalist.

"I said to him, 'Pretty much every year there are a [few players who become] millionaires out of Tour school,'" Doyle recalled. "'So why don't we be those two?'"

Fleisher won the first two events of 1998 and Doyle won the fourth. The following year, in 1999, Doyle won four times, including the Senior PGA Championship, and was third on the money list. Then, in 2001, after winning twice—including the Ford Senior Players Championship—and finishing second five times, he won the inaugural Charles Schwab Cup and donated the entire $1 million annuity to charity.

Doyle is as unassuming as they come. When he's not playing in a tournament, you can find him at his driving range in LaGrange, passing the time with the regulars and watching golf on TV.

"You hang around and you shoot the breeze and it's a good place to be. I don't ever look way in advance and dream," says Doyle about his philosophy of life. "You take care of today and when tomorrow comes, you take care of tomorrow."

Doyle captured the Charles Schwab Cup after winning the 2001 Ford Senior Players Championship during his highest money-making year on the Champions Tour.

In one of his nine Champions Tour victories, Doyle shot a final round 64 to win the 1999 Senior PGA Championship by two shots at the PGA National Golf Course in Florida.

Bruce Fleisher was slated for stardom as a 19-year-old when he won the U.S. Amateur Golf Championship in 1968 at Scioto Country Club in Columbus, Ohio.

Bruce Fleisher

Bruce Fleisher was one of those young, can't-miss amateurs. After winning the 1968 U.S. Amateur, the PGA TOUR was supposed to be his oyster. Instead, he waited to blossom until after he joined the Champions Tour.

Fleisher played the PGA TOUR from 1972 until 1984, but could only manage a couple of second-place finishes. He moved away from the TOUR in 1980 when his wife, Wendy, almost died giving birth to their daughter Jessica. He played fewer and fewer matches until he quit the TOUR in 1984 to take a club pro job in Miami. When he won the 1989 PGA Club Pro Championship, however, Fleisher decided to return and play on what was then the Hogan Tour. From there, he made his way back to the PGA TOUR.

In his first start, Fleisher won the 1991 New England Classic in a suspense-filled seven-hole playoff with Ian Baker-Finch. Fleisher ended things on the seventh extra hole with

Fleisher's career blossomed after he turned 50. Today, he is one of the most successful Champions Tour players in history.

Bruce Fleisher

First player to win his first two starts on the Champions Tour

* * *

Winner of the 1968 U.S. Amateur

* * *

Turned professional: 1969

* * *

PGA TOUR victories: One

* * *

Champions Tour victories: 18, including one U.S. Senior Open

a dramatic 50-foot birdie putt to complete the Cinderella tale.

Fleisher played the PGA TOUR for the next six years, continually working on his game with the Champions Tour foremost in his mind. He finished second to Allen Doyle in the 1998 Champions Tour Qualifying Tournament. He was the eighth player in Tour history to win in his Champions Tour debut and was the first player to win his first two events, winning the Royal Caribbean Classic and American Express Invitational in back-to-back weeks. He went on to win five more times that season. He also led the money list with $2,515,705, earned Player and Rookie of the Year honors, and led the Tour in scoring.

And he didn't stop there. Fleisher kept rolling, winning four times in 2000 and three times in 2001, including his only major, the 2001 U.S. Senior Open. That Sunday, he stared down Jack Nicklaus, fired a closing 68, and joined the Golden Bear and Arnold Palmer as one of the only three players to win both a U.S. Amateur and a U.S. Senior Open.

The quintessential late bloomer, Fleisher, who won just $1.7 million over his entire PGA TOUR career, now has 18 Champions Tour victories and ranks eighth on the Champions Tour all-time money leaders list with more than $13.7 million.

Fleisher sweetened an already lucrative senior career with his first major championship on the Champions Tour.

Raymond Floyd is one of the
most tenacious competitors in
golf history, as evidenced by his
piercing stare.

Raymond Floyd

He had a stare that could freeze the most hardened caddie or reporter. The stare was a sign that he was "on"—it was a tunnel vision that meant nothing existed except him, his club, and the hole. Once, in a major championship, when he was in such a state, he stared straight at his wife, Maria, and claimed he never saw her.

Such intensity exemplified Raymond Floyd's career and rewarded him with four major PGA TOUR championships—a Masters, a U.S. Open, and two PGA Championships. And in three of those majors, he demonstrated why almost no one was a better—or more deserving— front-runner.

At the 1969 PGA Championship, he led from start to finish and set what at the time was the record low 18-hole score: 65. At the 1976 Masters, he tied Jack Nicklaus's 72-hole total of 271—17-under-par—and beat the field by a then-record eight strokes. And at the 1982 PGA Championship, he opened with a 63 that he called "the best round of golf I've played any-where." From there, he captured his third major.

Floyd became the oldest winner of a major championship at the time by winning the 1986 U.S. Open at Shinnecock Hills at age 43. The previous week, he had shot a final-round 77 at the Westchester Classic, blowing the lead on Sunday. During the three-hour drive from Westchester to Southampton, site of the Open, his wife, Maria, gave him a stern pep talk. The results are self-evident: Floyd shot 66 in the final round to win by two shots.

In the months before Floyd turned 50, he won his third Doral-Ryder Open, beating Fred

Jack Nicklaus helps Floyd adjust his green jacket after Floyd's record-setting victory at the 1976 Masters.

Couples and Keith Clearwater by two shots. That victory came just two weeks after the Floyds' Indian Creek house had been destroyed by fire.

"I told Maria I wasn't going to play," he said. "We've got all these insurance adjustors and everything. We've got to figure out what we're going to do. She says, 'No. I'm going to handle all that. You go play. We need some positive stuff in the family. Go out and have a good tournament.' And Cinderella. . . I go win the golf tournament. Doral. At 49 years old." It was his third Doral title; with it, he joined Sam Snead as one of only two players to win at least one PGA TOUR event in four different decades.

Floyd was the new kid on the senior block in September 1992, and everyone knew there was a good chance he could run whatever table he wanted. Unlike some others, Floyd didn't win his debut. Instead, he won in his second start. After competing in his first senior event in Lexington, Kentucky, Floyd won the GTE North, beating Mike Hill by two shots. In a sweeping gesture, Floyd donated his $67,500 winner's check to help the victims of Hurricane Andrew, which had just blown through Florida.

Raymond Floyd

One of only two players to win official PGA TOUR events in four decades

* * *

Turned professional: 1961

* * *

PGA TOUR victories: 22, including two PGA Championships, one Masters, and one U.S. Open

* * *

Champions Tour victories: 14, including two Ford Senior Players Championships, one Senior PGA Championship, and one JELD-WEN Tradition

* * *

Inducted into the World Golf Hall of Fame in 1989

WORLD GOLF
HALL
of
FAME

The win also made Floyd the first player to win on both the PGA TOUR and the senior circuit in the same season. He won twice more on the Champions Tour after that, including the season-ending Senior Tour Championship.

As for winning on two tours? He claimed it was because he was still so active on the PGA TOUR. "It's not really a great big deal," he said. "I've been the only one really to have the chance.

Floyd's 1969 PGA Championship victory at NCR Country Club in Ohio was the first of his four major championship wins.

"Golf puts a man's character on the anvil and his richest qualities—patience, poise, and restraint—to the flame." —RAYMOND FLOYD

If Jack Nicklaus had played more golf [on his way to age 50], he might have."

In 1993, at age 51, he made the decision to play part-time on both tours and became the oldest player in Ryder Cup history. As one of Tom Watson's captain's picks, Floyd was responsible for the winning point. It was his eighth appearance.

"I think fitness had a great deal to do with it and I think it was goals, too," Floyd said. "I'm still a firm believer that part of the aging process is mental. I think it's a combination. And as your strength and physical attributes decline, your mental side is going up rapidly. And when they meet, they complement each other."

Floyd finished second on the money list in 1994 and 1995 and has 14 official victories to his credit. And while aches and pains have limited his practice time, he still loves to get out and play.

An exuberant Floyd celebrates after winning the Senior PGA Championship in 1995, one of four major wins on the Champions Tour.

Floyd, who owns one of the best short games in golf, can hole almost any shot from off the green.

In 2004, the 59-year-old Irwin bested 50-year-old Jay Haas to win his fourth Senior PGA Championship with a birdie on the final hole.

Hale Irwin

He never seems to get older, just better. The best senior player in the game just won't slow down. Through 2004, Hale Irwin amassed 40 Champions Tour wins, more than $26 million in earnings, two Charles Schwab Cups, four Senior PGA Championships, three Player of the Year Awards, and a remarkable record of top finishes.

Irwin amassed 20 victories during his PGA TOUR career—including three U.S. Opens—and gained a reputation for being able to win at the toughest courses golf had to offer. He won three times at Harbour Town, including his first victory at the Heritage Classic in 1971. He won at Butler National when it hosted the Western Open in 1975. He won the Memorial at Muirfield Village in 1983.

And of course there were the three U.S. Open titles. The first came in 1974 at Winged Foot during what was later called "The Massacre at Winged Foot." Irwin won the title with a 7-over-par total of 287, the highest winning score in years. He hit what he would term his favorite shot on the 72nd hole: a 2-iron that wound up 20 feet and two putts from the hole.

Irwin became the first player to match par during a 72-hole championship when he won the 1979 Open at Inverness. After a course-record 67 in the third round, Irwin built a six-shot lead going into the final nine holes and ended up winning by two.

At Medinah in 1990, he made a 50-foot putt on the final hole to draw even with Mike Donald, whom he would beat in a playoff the next day. After

Irwin, at age 45, celebrates his 50-foot birdie putt on the 18th green in 1990, which forced a playoff the next day. It would be his third, and most famous, U.S. Open title.

Irwin's high winning score at the 1974 U.S. Open led television broadcaster Dick Schaop to dub the event "The Massacre at Winged Foot."

Irwin won the second of his three
U.S. Open titles in 1979 at
Inverness.

he made the putt, Irwin, circling the green on a dead run, slapped fives with the gallery—one of golf's most enduring images. His third U.S. Open victory, which made him the only player with exactly three titles, came at age 45, another testament to his athletic longevity.

When Irwin turned 50, he redefined the senior game. Joining halfway through the 1995 season, he played like a man a decade younger. After winning four events in his first 18 months as a senior, he went on a two-year streak, winning 16 times, earning $5.3 million, and setting a scoring record in 1998 of 68.58 that may last for decades.

How dominant has Irwin been? He hasn't dropped out of the top five list of money winners since his half-season in 1995. He has a $7 million lead over Gil Morgan on the all-time money list, and his 40 Champions Tour wins leave him 11 ahead of second-place Lee Trevino.

In 1997, at age 52, he had a Hale of a season. After winning just four events in his first two senior seasons, Irwin took off. No one could touch him. Not even Gil Morgan, who won six times and finished second four more. Irwin won nine times and enjoyed the first $2 million senior season.

Irwin's spectacular nine victories started off with a two-shot win over Morgan in the MasterCard

Championship in January. His run ended in October when he beat Bruce Summerhays and Mike Hill by three shots to capture the Hyatt Regency Maui Kaanapali Classic and equal Peter Thomson's 1985 senior record for number of wins in a season.

"I think I'm a more complete player," he explained at the close of 1997. "There's no reluctance now if I have to play a certain shape of a shot. As a result I'm hitting my irons closer than ever. My putting is improved, particularly in the crunch. I'm a little bit longer and straighter off the tee, and that's mostly technology. I think I'm managing my game better than ever. I still see in myself an ability to learn, and a willingness."

But his victories were never routine. Just look at the sixth victory in the string. Irwin watched a

One of Irwin's two U.S. Senior Open titles came in 2000 at Saucon Valley Country Club in Pennsylvania.

Hale Irwin

The oldest player to win the U.S. Open, at age 45

* * *

Turned professional: 1968

* * *

PGA TOUR victories: 20, including three U.S. Opens

* * *

Champions Tour victories: 40, including four Senior PGA Championships, two U.S. Senior Opens, and one Ford Senior Players Championship

* * *

Inducted into the World Golf Hall of Fame in 1992

WORLD GOLF
HALL
of
FAME

"If you're not just a little bit nervous before a match, you probably don't have the expectations of yourself you should have." —HALE IRWIN

two-stroke lead disappear on the back nine at the 1997 BankBoston Classic and then made a 50-foot snaking birdie at the 17th hole on Sunday to give him a two-stroke win over Jerry McGee and Bob Wynn.

"The 17th couldn't have gotten a whole lot more exciting for me than it was," Irwin said. "The competition is such a part of my lifeblood. The thrill of the chase is so great that this will go down big in my mind."

Irwin won seven times in 1998 and led the money list, then added five more wins in 1999 and was second on the money list. Irwin stepped up again in 2002, winning four times and setting another Champions Tour record in earnings with $3,028,304.

In 2004, at 59, he won his fourth Senior PGA Championship, his second Charles Schwab Cup, and finished second—less than $300,000— behind Craig Stadler on the money list. Overall, he has finished in the top three 98 times in 235 events.

Most players his age have slowed down and lost a step. Not Irwin. No one would be surprised to see him remain at the top well into his 60s. "My attitude," he said in 1998, "isn't one [that's] half-empty, it's half-full and how to make it fuller. How that manifests itself on the golf course? I just think it speaks for itself."

Through 2004, Irwin won 40 tournaments on the Champions Tour, including the 1997 Senior PGA Championship.

Hale Irwin, who claimed the U.S. Senior Open title in 1998, is far and away the most successful Champions Tour player in its 25-year history.

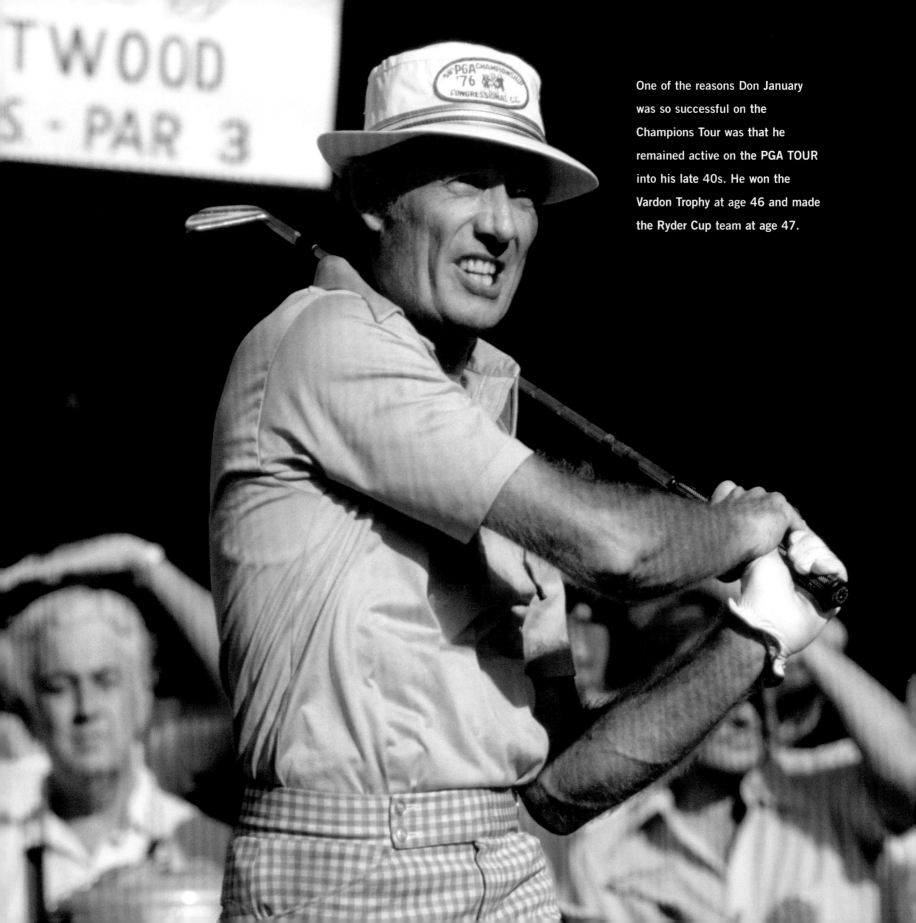

One of the reasons Don January was so successful on the Champions Tour was that he remained active on the PGA TOUR into his late 40s. He won the Vardon Trophy at age 46 and made the Ryder Cup team at age 47.

Don January

He was never a man in a hurry. He was built like a 1-iron and walked as smoothly as he swung a club, but in slow motion. One day when an amateur partner shanked a shot straight at him, January put his hand up and batted the wayward ball toward the pin. "Downhill slope," he drawled.

The lanky Texan—known as "Bones" to most and "Old Folks" to Sam Snead—had the perfect temperament and pace for golf, winning ten times on the PGA TOUR. His finest moment came at the 1967 PGA Championship at Columbine Country Club in Colorado, where he won the title by beating

Don Massengale by two shots in an 18-hole playoff. Six years earlier he had just missed a second major, losing the 1961 PGA Championship by one shot in a playoff to Jerry Barber, despite shooting 68 in the playoff.

January remained competitive on the PGA TOUR in his 40s. At age 46, he had his best year on the TOUR when he won the MONY Tournament of Champions and the Vardon Trophy for lowest scoring average.

When he turned 50, he turned his attention to extending his career by helping to launch the senior circuit. As one of the Senior Six—the original

January won the Senior PGA Championship and 21 other Champions Tour events during his senior career.

members of the Tour—January helped organize the fledgling Tour, then dominated it, leading the money list for three of the first five years and finishing second to old Texas pal Miller Barber the other two years.

Everyone eligible showed up for the senior debut on June 20 at the links-style Atlantic City Country Club. It was only fitting that January started what would be a great five-year run by beating Mike Souchak by two shots.

January finished in the top four on the money list in 1985 and 1986 and won the last of his 22 Champions Tour titles the following season at the MONY Senior Tournament of Champions. He also won the Liberty Mutual Legends of Golf three times—in 1982 with Sam Snead and in 1985 and 1986 with Gene Littler—and he won a record 35 Grand Champions events.

When January retired in 1999, Bruce Devlin said, "He was one of our leaders. Whenever you wanted an example of how to handle yourself on and off the golf course, he had to be on that list. He was a gentleman." January believed he was one of the fortunate. "I'll tell you what this game means to me," he said. "I've never worked a day in my life."

Don January

One of the founding members of the Champions Tour

* * *

Shares the record at three for most eagles in a Champions Tour round

* * *

Turned professional: 1956

* * *

PGA TOUR victories: 10, including one PGA Championship

* * *

Champions Tour victories: 22, including one Senior PGA Championship

January, who retired from competitive golf after 43 years, was the first to break the $1 million mark in Champions Tour earnings.

In 1981, Nelson won the PGA Championship, the first of three major titles, with a four-stroke victory at the Atlanta Athletic Club in his home state of Georgia.

Larry Nelson

Larry Nelson is arguably the greatest player in the game most people don't really know. He put himself through school and didn't take up the game of golf until he was 21, after he had served a tour of duty in Vietnam, posted near the hot spot of Da Nang. In fact, he had never played a single round of golf until he hurt his pitching arm playing baseball. It was as if golf had been waiting for him all along. Within a year he was breaking 70. In four years he was playing on the PGA TOUR, and in his second event, he tied for eighth at the Greater Jacksonville Open.

"If somebody wrote [my] story and they put it on the screen, they'd say, 'Nah, it would never happen,'" Nelson said, putting his career into perspective. "I actually did it. If it were done now, a guy goes over to Iraq and fights, comes back, starts playing golf, and wins the U.S. Open in, say, 2012; it would be a terrific story. But then, it wasn't that big a deal."

Nelson is quiet, soft-spoken, and gentle. He has been married for 37 years to his high school sweetheart, Gayle. He is the only three-time major winner not in the World Golf Hall of Fame. He is the only player to go 5-0 in a single Ryder Cup match and, considering he has a career 9-3-1 record in the matches, he is one of the few outstanding Ryder Cup players never honored as a captain. Yet he's a man who has a calm and peace about him. A man who honestly doesn't need the spotlight that has eluded him his entire career.

Those majors, which everyone seems to forget, are the 1981 and 1987 PGA Championships and

Nelson has won 19 tournaments on the Champions Tour, including the 2004 Administaff Small Business Classic.

Nelson beat two of the greatest players in the game—Seve Ballesteros and Tom Watson—to win the U.S. Open title at Oakmont Country Club in 1983.

the 1983 U.S. Open. He won the 1981 PGA Championship over Fuzzy Zoeller at the Atlanta Athletic Club and won the 1987 PGA Championship in a playoff over Lanny Wadkins at PGA National in Florida. In each, Nelson was considered a surprise winner—especially at the 1983 Open.

That year, the final round at Oakmont Country Club in western Pennsylvania had been billed as an epic duel between Tom Watson and Seve Ballesteros, two of the game's greats. Nelson was one shot back, but no one gave him much thought, despite having birdied seven of his last 11 holes for a 6-under 65 in the third round.

Instead, all eyes were on the featured pairing. Watson blistered the front nine with a 5-under-31, while Ballesteros fell aside. Nelson, with a 3-under 33 of his own on the front side, was three behind with nine to play.

Larry Nelson

Holds the Champions Tour record for most consecutive rounds at par or less, with 32 in 2000

* * *

Turned professional: 1971

* * *

PGA TOUR victories: 10, including two PGA Championships and one U.S. Open

* * *

Champions Tour victories: 19

Watson became unglued with bogeys at the 10th and 12th, and Nelson caught him with a birdie at the 14th. One hole later, play was suspended because of a thunderstorm, and the players were forced to come back on Monday.

Nelson took the lead with a 60-foot birdie putt at the 16th, but three-putted the 18th to come in at 280, 4-under par. Watson bogeyed the 17th to fall one behind and could only manage a par at the last, giving the title to Nelson.

As a senior, Nelson still takes a backseat to the likes of Hale Irwin and Craig Stadler. He won ten PGA TOUR events, but has nearly doubled that on the Champions Tour. Nelson has won 19 times, six of them coming in an incredible 2000 season when he won four of his last eight starts and walked off with Player of the Year honors and the money title. Nelson finished in the top four on the money list his first four full seasons and is third on the Champions Tour career money list with $12,023,819. Only Hale Irwin ($20,592,965) and Gil Morgan ($14,319,252) have won more. And, yes, he's still overlooked.

Nelson was Champions Tour Player of the Year in 2000 with six victories, including four in his last eight starts.

Larry Nelson celebrates a putt at the 2000 JELD-WEN Tradition. His phenomenal year spurred the Associated Press to dub him "Senior Tiger."

Jack Nicklaus hugs the 1975 PGA Championship cup. Nicklaus's strategy on the greens was simple: "I never went in to a tournament thinking I had to beat a certain player. I had to beat the golf course."

Jack Nicklaus

Jack William Nicklaus is easily the best player who has ever lived. But it's not only because of his 18 major championship wins, although they certainly set him apart. His superstar status comes from Nicklaus's total domination of the PGA TOUR for longer than anyone could have imagined.

The closest anyone has ever come to matching Nicklaus's number of championship victories was the great Bobby Jones, who recorded 13 majors in his short career, having virtually retired by age 28. Like Jones, Nicklaus was great—consistently great. From the time he won his first event, the 1962 U.S. Open,

Nicklaus racked up 73 PGA TOUR victories, second only to Sam Snead's 81. And he finished second an incredible 19 times.

Nicklaus won at least two tournaments per year from 1962 to 1978. Fourteen of those 17 years, he won at least three events, and seven times he won five or more. Twice he won seven tournaments in a season and those came in back-to-back years, 1972 and 1973. In doing so, he beat the best the game had to offer.

He went up against Arnold Palmer, Lee Trevino, and Tom Watson—all in their prime. The rivalry between Nicklaus and Palmer in the early-to-mid-1960s was legendary; it began when Palmer came from seven shots behind to beat Nicklaus, then an amateur, at the 1960 U.S. Open at Cherry Hills. Ben Hogan, who was paired with the 20-year-old Nicklaus, pointed at him and told the press that he was the one who should have won the championship.

Two years later, after Nicklaus had turned professional, he and Palmer squared off at the 1962

Nicklaus had the perfect game for Augusta National—he hit it high and long—and won the first of his six Masters titles in 1963.

U.S. Open at Oakmont Country Club. Nicklaus shot a final-round 69 to tie Palmer and send the matter into an 18-hole playoff the next day, which Nicklaus won by three shots. From there, it seemed that for the next few years both Nicklaus and Palmer were in the fray at The Masters.

Palmer won The Masters in 1962, Nicklaus in '63, Palmer in '64, and Nicklaus in '65 and '66. When Palmer won in '64, Nicklaus tied for second. When Nicklaus won in '65, Palmer tied for second. At Nicklaus's 1966 victory, Palmer tied for fourth, two shots out of a three-way playoff.

In all, Nicklaus won six Masters titles, the most memorable of which came in 1986, when at age 46, he shocked and delighted those in the gallery with a classic come-from-behind victory. Nicklaus shot a 6-under-par 30 on the final nine holes on Sunday, including an eagle at the par-5 15th and a near hole-in-one at the par-3 16th to beat third-round leader Greg Norman.

Nicklaus won the U.S. Open four times, and has claimed three British Open titles and five PGA Championships. He is the only player in history to win all four Grand Slam titles at least three times each. No one else has won all four even twice. He played in six Ryder Cup matches, captained two U.S. teams, and was a 1974 inaugural member of the World Golf Hall of Fame.

Ironically, the times he finished second were in the tournaments for which he is best known. In 1977, Nicklaus hooked up with Watson in an epic duel at the British Open at Turnberry. He shot 65-66 on the

As an amateur, Nicklaus almost won the 1960 U.S. Open at Cherry Hills near Denver.

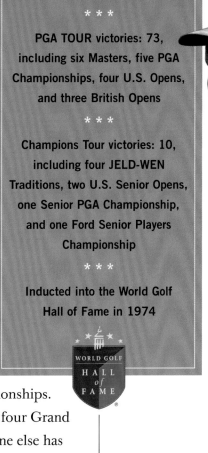

Jack Nicklaus

First to win all four majors twice

* * *

Winner of the 1959 and 1961 U.S. Amateurs

* * *

Turned professional: 1961

* * *

PGA TOUR victories: 73, including six Masters, five PGA Championships, four U.S. Opens, and three British Opens

* * *

Champions Tour victories: 10, including four JELD-WEN Traditions, two U.S. Senior Opens, one Senior PGA Championship, and one Ford Senior Players Championship

* * *

Inducted into the World Golf Hall of Fame in 1974

WORLD GOLF
HALL
of
FAME

The most famous of Nicklaus's Masters victories came in 1986, at age 46, with son Jackie as his caddie.

weekend but lost by a shot to Watson, who shot 65-65. Even so, Nicklaus holed a 40-foot birdie on the 72nd hole, forcing Watson to make a five-footer to win.

When he turned 50 in 1990, he didn't commit to many senior events, but he started his second career with a flourish. He won the first senior event he entered, The Tradition at Desert Mountain, and fittingly, it was designated a senior major. He also won the Senior Players Championship that year, finished second to Lee Trevino at the U.S. Senior Open, and was third at the Senior PGA Championship.

Trevino said the only way to beat Nicklaus at his best was "to hope Jack broke his ankle or signed the wrong scorecard." Nicklaus did neither at Dearborn Country Club in Michigan at the Senior Players Championship. Instead, the Golden Bear got into the same groove he had found at Augusta National in 1986 and walked away owning the lowest 72-hole score in Champions Tour history after shooting a 27-under-par 261.

He needed just 111 putts at the Senior Tournament Players Championship, many of them

Nicklaus triumphantly hoists the trophy presented to him at the 1980 U.S. Open.

20-footers, and found himself putting for an eagle 11 times out of 16 at the par-5s over the four days. "I don't think I've ever putted like this any other time in my career," he said.

The following year, he entered five senior events and won three, including the U.S. Senior Open. In all, Nicklaus won 10 events on the Champions Tour, eight of them majors.

Everyone hoped he would play more, but back pains and a hip replacement in 1999 kept him from competing as much as he wanted. His golf course design business and other enterprises also kept him busy, although he still competed on a limited basis on the PGA TOUR. Even then, he closed with a 65 to tie for sixth at the 1998 Masters at age 58.

By 2004, at age 64, he was hinting at retirement. "I don't think my golf game is good enough to play anymore," he said. "It doesn't make any difference if it's a major championship or anywhere. When your ability is leaving you, then you go do something else."

Nicklaus greets his fans in 1996 after his fourth and final victory at the JELD-WEN Tradition.

Even at age 65, Nicklaus competed in a few select events on the PGA TOUR, especially his signature tournament—the Memorial—at Muirfield Village Golf Club near his hometown of Columbus, Ohio.

Arnold Palmer, waiting to tee off on the 10th hole at Augusta National in 1971, was a formidable opponent at The Masters, having won the championship four times from 1958 to 1964.

Arnold Palmer

Anyone who has ever seen Arnold Palmer remembers the first time they saw him wink or hitch up his pants or wind up and smack a golf ball and walk down the fairway with his shirttail flapping. Anyone who has ever seen Arnold Palmer in person knows without a doubt that he is, quite simply, the King.

As Gary Player said, Arnie fell out of bed with charisma. There was no learning it or cultivating it. He was the people's choice from the first time he stepped onto the course. At every course on which he played, whether major championship or off-season Skins Game, he was electric and everyone knew it.

Palmer's father, Deacon, was the pro and superintendent at Latrobe Country Club in Pennsylvania, and young Arnie grew up around the pro shop and the driving range. When he was a teenager, he was given a job in the shop, but would sneak out to the range periodically, much to the consternation of his father.

All that stealth paid off as Palmer went on to star at Wake Forest and earn his first major triumph

Palmer's legion of fans—dubbed "Arnie's Army"—make him the most beloved player in the world.

at the 1954 U.S Amateur. He turned professional later that year and launched his PGA TOUR career with a victory at the 1955 Canadian Open.

Three years later he won the first of four Masters championships, just a few days after Ben Hogan wondered aloud how the devil this Palmer kid got into the field. He won three more Masters titles—in 1960, 1962, and 1964—to go along with consecutive British Open championships in 1961 and 1962, the 1960 U.S. Open, and 55 other PGA TOUR titles. He is considered responsible for single-handedly reviving the British Open, traveling overseas when not many Americans did, thereby elevating that venerable championship to be on par with The Masters, U.S. Open, and PGA Championship.

Perhaps none of his tournament victories tells his complete story so well as the 1960 U.S. Open. Palmer entered the final round at Cherry Hills Country Club near Denver seven shots out of the lead. Before the round, in the locker room, he surmised to a couple of sportswriters that if he shot a four-round total of 280, he could win. That meant he needed 65 on Sunday.

He remarked to the writers, Dan Jenkins and Bob Drum, that if he could drive the first green—which he had tried to do all week—he might shoot a good enough score on the outward nine to put him in contention. Both Jenkins and Drum scoffed at the strategy and Palmer, miffed, stormed to the first tee. In typical Palmer style, he drove the first green and shot 30 on the front nine on his way to a two-stroke victory over then-amateur Jack Nicklaus.

The last of Palmer's Masters titles was especially sweet as he beat defending champion Jack Nicklaus and Dave Marr by six shots in 1964 to become the first player to win four Masters titles.

During Palmer's career, he became the first player on the PGA TOUR to earn more than $100,000 in a season, doing so in 1962, when he won eight times. He was also the first to reach the $1 million mark in career winnings, in 1968. In 1980 the TOUR named the annual award for the leading money winner after Palmer.

The way he transformed the game should make every player on the PGA TOUR grateful. Palmer is the main reason players compete for such big purses today. He took what was once viewed as an elitist game, personalized it, and brought it into the television era. And along with increased television coverage came more money flowing into the TOUR from sponsors.

Palmer's fan appeal is legendary. He is perhaps the most beloved player of the modern era. He always made it a point to make eye contact with every fan he encountered, leading each and every one to believe he or she was special. He frowned, grimaced,

Palmer tees off among the crowd on the 6th hole at the 1966 Masters. His unusual approach to golf led one broadcaster to remark, "In a sport that was high society, he made it *High Noon*."

and jumped for joy. The fact that he was unafraid to show his emotions registered with the gallery. His triumphs were their triumphs and his failures were theirs, too. Fans related to that rumpled shirt and loopy swing. They loved his Pennsylvania roots and his grace under pressure. They loved the way he made them feel as if they were just as important a part of his round as a 12-foot downhill twister at the 72nd hole.

Even in the Tiger Woods era, Palmer always draws the biggest galleries. Young and old alike flock to watch the King perform, even if he doesn't play anywhere near the way he once did. All are hoping for a glimpse, a grin, a pumped fist. They all want to be able to say they saw Arnold Palmer in person.

In one of the game's most capricious twists of fate, Arnie came up just one championship short of the ultimate career milestone—the career Grand Slam—because he never won a PGA Championship. So it was only fitting that his senior debut and first senior victory should come at the 1980 Senior PGA Championship. That moment brought the senior circuit from a struggling question mark to must-see entertainment. Arnie's presence on the course ushered in a new era—one

Arnold Palmer

Tied with Jack Nicklaus for most consecutive years winning at least one tournament with 17

* * *

Winner of the 1954 U.S. Amateur

* * *

Turned professional: 1954

* * *

PGA TOUR victories: 62, including four Masters, two British Opens, and one U.S. Open

* * *

Champions Tour victories: 10, including two Senior PGA Championships, two Ford Senior Players Championships, and one U.S. Senior Open

* * *

Inducted into the World Golf Hall of Fame in 1974

WORLD GOLF
HALL
of
FAME

filled with gallery ropes, a crush of fans, corporate sponsors, and television contracts.

Along the way he won 10 Champions Tour events, including a U.S. Senior Open in 1981, another Senior PGA Championship in 1984, and two Ford Senior Players Championships. Palmer was an inaugural selection for the World Golf Hall of Fame in 1974 and was elected to the PGA Hall of Fame in 1980. He played on six Ryder Cup teams and has captained both the Ryder Cup and The Presidents Cup. He played his final Masters in 2004.

He plays only a handful of events today, but any time he is in the field, he draws big crowds. It doesn't matter what Arnie shoots or where he finishes, fans turn out to see the man who personalized the game not once but twice—all with a wink, a hitch of his pants, a patented charge, and an ageless grace.

Palmer returned to glory as a senior, winning the U.S. Senior Open Championship in 1981 at Canterbury Golf Club outside Cleveland.

Arnold Palmer was still a magnetic presence during the 1993 U.S. Senior Open at Cherry Hills in Englewood, Colorado, where he won the 1960 U.S. Open.

Gary Player, being interviewed at the 1959 Masters, came to America to become one of the greatest golfers in history. Two years later, he would win his first green jacket.

Gary Player

We know him as the man in black. The wiry South African loves old westerns and those movies inspired him to wear entirely black outfits—the bad guy color. Fans thought it was all too appropriate. Gary Player always seemed to be trying to knock off heroes like Arnold Palmer or Jack Nicklaus. And he traveled millions of miles to do it.

Player was the first global golfer. He dominated in South Africa, then took his game to Europe, where he became the youngest British Open champion in history, winning the 1959 championship at Muirfield at age 24.

Player became one of professional golf's "Big Three" with Arnold Palmer (left) and Jack Nicklaus (right). Together, they would dominate golf in the 1960s.

This victory marked the beginning of a World Golf Hall of Fame career and the beginning of his role in the game as one of the "Big Three"— with Nicklaus, Palmer, and Player. The trio would dominate world golf in the 1960s and Player certainly contributed his share. He won The Masters in 1961 and the PGA Championship in 1962. Three years later, he beat Palmer to win the 1965 U.S. Open and become the third man—and one of only four in history—to win the career Grand Slam.

He won his second British Open in 1968 and his second PGA Championship four years later. In 1974, he won two majors—The Masters and his third British Open. In 1978, at age 43, he had perhaps his greatest triumph, his third Masters title. He started the final round seven shots behind Saturday leader Hubert Green. Player shot an 8-under-par 64 in the final round, including six birdies on the back nine, to win by a shot.

In all, he won 10 majors and 24 PGA TOUR events and had 53 international victories. Player did it circling the globe and searching for perfection on and off the course. He believed in Ben Hogan's theory of practice: you never could get enough. He was the same when it came to physical fitness. Player's

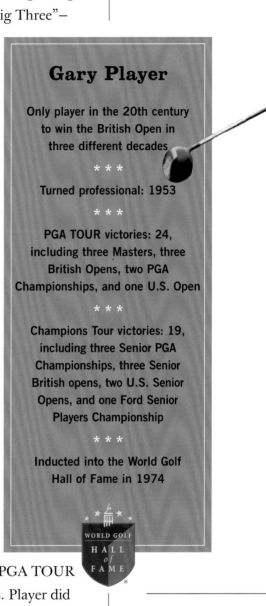

Gary Player

Only player in the 20th century to win the British Open in three different decades

* * *

Turned professional: 1953

* * *

PGA TOUR victories: 24, including three Masters, three British Opens, two PGA Championships, and one U.S. Open

* * *

Champions Tour victories: 19, including three Senior PGA Championships, three Senior British opens, two U.S. Senior Opens, and one Ford Senior Players Championship

* * *

Inducted into the World Golf Hall of Fame in 1974

WORLD GOLF
HALL
of
FAME

The defending champion, Player treated fans to some flashy slacks while practicing for the 1960 British Open.

regimen was uncompromising, which meant that when he turned 50 and started playing on the Champions Tour, he was playing with a body a decade younger than everyone else's.

He summed up his drive for excellence in his 1991 autobiography: "What I have learned about myself is that I am an animal when it comes to achievement and wanting success. There is never enough success for me." In that relentless pursuit of greatness, he overcame a number of obstacles. He was not large in stature and, therefore, not long off the tee. His grip was too strong and his swing too flat. But he had a brilliant short game and was perhaps the world's greatest bunker player. And he always seemed to make the big putt at the right time.

Player couldn't wait to turn 50 and try his hand at the Champions Tour. He was like a race-horse headed for the starting gate. His birthday was on November 1, 1985, which left him just one event to play on the Champions Tour after celebrating his

Player, who teed it up all over the world in his career, jokingly challenges Chi Chi Rodriguez to take a practice swing.

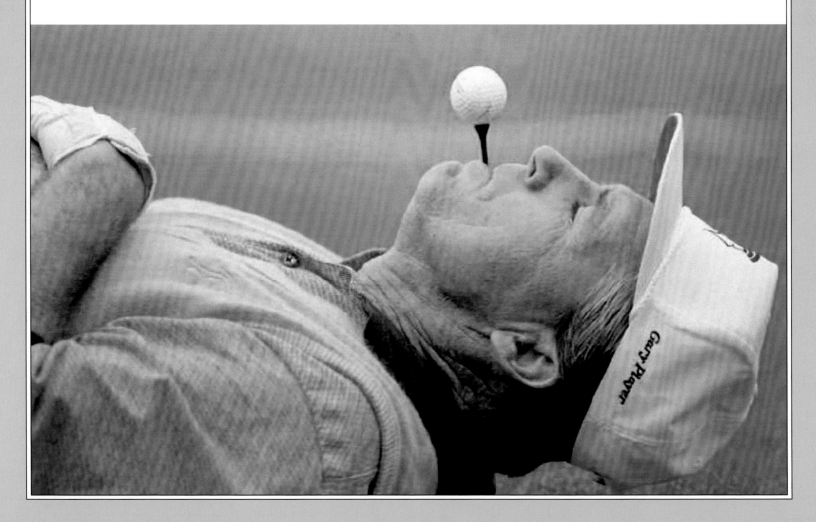

Player relished playing under the toughest conditions, as evidenced by his three British Open championships.

{ "The harder you work, the luckier you get." —GARY PLAYER }

new senior status. That was the 1985 Quadel Senior Classic, which he promptly won. He won three times the second season, including the first of six majors.

Five years, 13 tournament wins, and four senior majors later, Player faced down Jack Nicklaus and Lee Trevino at Palm Beach Gardens, Florida, and won his final major title at the 1990 Senior PGA Championship. Player not only defeated his two younger playing partners, Nicklaus and Trevino, but also overcame inclement weather for this victory. Nicklaus, the new kid on this block, opened with a 68, took a three-shot lead, and looked nearly unbeatable on what, essentially, was a course that was all of ten minutes from his driveway. Then came Friday and a second-round 78.

"I found out today I am human," said Nicklaus after that round. "The worst news is that somebody else might find out."

Perhaps one of his old rivals? Player jumped on it, shooting 29 on the front nine Saturday morning to take a five-shot lead over Nicklaus—and six

over Trevino—into the final round. He persevered through two rain delays and near darkness in the final round to win his third Senior PGA Championship, saying, "I was a little like Ray Charles playing

those last three holes. I couldn't see a thing."

Player kept winning into his 60s, his last victory coming at the 1998 Northville Long Island Classic. He also won 11 Grand Champions events and a dozen more unofficial events, including three Senior British Opens. His signature black clothing earned him the nickname of the Black Knight, which became the logo for his business, Black Knight International.

Player's Senior PGA Championship win in 1990 at Rancho Park, California, was the last of his six senior majors.

Player chips out of a sand trap during the 1994 Senior British Open. No bunker shot was too daunting for Player, who is considered the greatest bunker player in history.

Dana Quigley, who played briefly on the PGA TOUR, turned from club professional into an unqualified competitive success on the Champions Tour.

Dana Quigley

Dana Quigley always addresses the first insect that circles his golf ball each day with a "Hi, Dad." It's a game he plays every day to remind himself that his father is there watching over him.

Quigley lost his father the same day he won his first Champions Tour event. He called the victory the greatest moment in his golf career, but the incredible high of winning the 1997 Northville Long Island Classic was quickly replaced a few minutes later when he received the devastating news that his father had just passed away.

Quigley hadn't seen it coming. He had qualified on Monday, played in the Wednesday pro-am at Meadow Brook Golf Club, then drove home to Rhode Island and took his children to the hospital, where their grandfather was battling cancer. When Quigley came back to Long Island, he played one of the best rounds of his life. He led, he fell back, he stepped up and tied Jay Sigel, then holed a two-footer on the third playoff hole for his first win.

"It's funny that God would take his life and give me mine back in the same day," Quigley said after the tournament, with tears running down his face. "This is supposed to be my happiest moment ever. His dying will make me remember the day forever."

Friends told him the only way his dad could be with him that day was to die and be there in spirit. "I hung my hat on that," he said. "I want to believe it. I really feel he was there for that victory. Jay Sigel three-putted four greens of the last six and I figured my father was up there with

a hockey stick knocking the balls out. Someone was helping me. I wasn't doing it on my own."

The Rhode Island native, whose nephew Brett plays on the PGA TOUR, had great success in New England PGA section events when he was in his late 40s, winning 17 tournaments. At the age of 49, he turned to sports psychologist Bob Rotella to help him make the leap to the Champions Tour.

"All he did was get me to believe in myself," said Quigley, who was the head pro at Crestwood Country Club. "And evidently my game's good enough to handle it out here." It must be. Not only does Quigley tee it up just about every day, but he also plays every event he can. So far, that's been 262 consecutive starts for which he's been eligible and 248 straight events period.

Quigley has won eight Champions Tour events and more than $10.25 million in his first eight seasons and shows no signs of slowing down. "I can truly say there's not one thing out here I take for granted," he said. "I feel like someone gave me a free pass to go into a giant show and I'm still in there on a pass."

Dana Quigley

**Known as golf's "Iron Man,"
Quigley logs an ongoing Champions
Tour record for consecutive starts
that reached 262 at the end of
the 2004 season**

* * *

Turned professional: 1971

* * *

Champions Tour victories: Eight

Quigley celebrates after making his final putt to win the 2002 SBC Championship in San Antonio. Quigley plays every event for which he is eligible.

Playing his 250th consecutive event at the 2004 Ford Senior Players Championship, Quigley crosses a bridge on the 11th hole at the TPC of Michigan. In his first eight seasons, Quigley won eight tournaments and more than $10 million.

After sinking a birdie putt, natural showman Chi Chi Rodriguez entertains the gallery with his unique sword dance at the 1991 U.S. Senior Open at Oakland Hills Country Club. He eventually lost to Jack Nicklaus in a playoff.

Chi Chi Rodriguez

C hi Chi Rodriguez can't help himself. He's part entertainer, part Pied Piper. Galleries are drawn to the man with the trademark Panama hat who punctuates birdies by performing a sword dance with his putter and ends the dance by covering the hole with his hat, just in case the ball decides to hop out. He's also responsible for the famous line, "Jack Nicklaus has become a legend in his spare time."

Rodriguez grew up in poverty in Puerto Rico, eating beans and corn with his hands; his first golf club was a branch from a guava tree that he used to hit tin cans. His hands are slightly crooked from having had rickets as a child, but that didn't stop him from teaching himself the game or leaving behind youth baseball—he played with Roberto Clemente and Orlando Cepeda—and having a Hall of Fame golf career.

Rodriguez won only eight times on the PGA TOUR, but the crowds flocked to watch his creative shotmaking. He wasn't a consistent winner, but he still earned more than $1 million in his career. His first win came in 1963 at the Denver Open Invitational, his last at the 1979 Tallahassee Open.

He had a prolific senior career, however, winning 22 Champions Tour events, including two major championships—the 1986 Senior Tournament Players Championship and the 1987 Senior PGA Championship—earning more than $7 million.

In 1987, Rodriguez put himself in the record books with four consecutive victories. He started his run with a win at the Vantage At The Dominion and

Though slight of build, Rodriguez—seen here at the 1965 Thunderbird Tourney—packed a powerful punch in his younger days and was a creative shotmaker.

> "A golf ball is like a clock. Always hit it at 6 o'clock and make it go toward 12 o'clock. But make sure you're in the same time zone." —CHI CHI RODRIGUEZ

won the next two tournaments, at the United Hospitals Senior Golf Championship and the Silver Pages Classic. He did not play the next week, when Bruce Crampton won the Denver Champions of Golf, but then he came back to win the Reunion Pro-Am with a closing 65 to edge out Crampton by a shot. In doing so, Rodriguez broke the short-lived record of three tournament victories in a row set earlier that year by left-hander Bob Charles, who had won the Vintage Chrysler Invitational, the GTE Classic, and the Sunwest-Charley Pride Classic.

Rodriguez's streak began the week after Charles's third victory. Rodriguez holed a 25-footer for a birdie at the first hole and followed with a six-footer at the second to cut Crampton's lead to

Rodriguez loved curving the ball in both directions and hitting shots most people could only imagine, as he demonstrates here at the 1993 U.S. Senior Open at Cherry Hills Golf Course in Colorado.

one. Rodriguez scored another six-footer at the 10th hole, then chipped in at the 11th and pulled even at the 12th when he came close to holing an 80-foot bunker shot and settled for a birdie. He took the lead with a birdie at 17, the same hole Don January birdied the year before to beat him. In all, Rodriguez threw seven birdies and 11 pars at Crampton, who had led by three at the start of the day, and the Dallas resident couldn't counter.

"Everything was computerized," said Rodriguez. "I played those 18 holes in my mind last night about twice. I figured I had to shoot 65."

Rodriguez was certainly a financial success on the Champions Tour, but he also clearly enjoyed being part of the fan-friendly, entertainment aspect of the senior circuit. "Golf is show business," he said. "You're on a stage and you give your people a show."

Rodriguez, a member of the World Golf Hall of Fame and the World Humanitarian Sports Hall of Fame, was a natural at playing in outings and hosting clinics, and often did both to earn money between playing the PGA TOUR and the Champions Tour. He also had a generous charitable side. He was a soft touch and sometimes gave away more money than he earned. In 1979 he founded the Chi Chi Rodriguez Youth Foundation, which has raised more than $5 million to help abused and troubled children.

In 1986, he was awarded the Card Walker Award from the PGA TOUR for his considerable contributions to junior golf. He has remained true to his own motto and the standard he set for all golfers: "A man never stands taller than when he stoops to help a child."

Chi Chi Rodriguez

Holds the Champions Tour record for consecutive victories: Four

* * *

Turned professional: 1960

* * *

PGA TOUR victories: Eight

* * *

Champions Tour victories: 22, including one Senior PGA Championship and one Ford Senior Players Championship

* * *

Inducted into the World Golf Hall of Fame in 1992

WORLD GOLF
HALL
of
FAME

As much as he lives to entertain, Rodriguez also has a serious side, which manifests itself in his charitable work.

Rodriguez, practicing at Troon before the 1978 British Open, was always a tireless worker.

Charlie Sifford contemplates a shot over his trademark cigar at the 1997 Senior PGA Championship, 37 years after he became the first African American to play full time on the PGA TOUR.

Charlie Sifford

C harlie Sifford was seldom without one of his thick trademark cigars on the course. But that isn't why he got noticed. Sifford wanted to play golf, and he wasn't going to let a little thing like pervasive racism stop him. He fought to end the Caucasians-only clause, which prevented blacks from playing on the PGA TOUR. In 1960, he became the TOUR's first full-time black member. Through his efforts and the efforts of others, he broke the color line in golf, becoming the sport's own Jackie Robinson. But that was only the start of things for Sifford.

He got his thick skin from fighting in World War II. Sifford served in the infantry and was at the invasion of Okinawa. "The army made me tough as hell," he told the *Charlotte Observer*. "If it hadn't been for the army, I don't think I could have gone through this golf thing. In the army, you had to learn to live with somebody who didn't want you around." So Sifford lived his dream, getting his PGA TOUR card at the age of 38, dealing with his anger, and blocking out the racism. His courage inspired others like Pete Brown and Lee Elder to follow.

Sifford was 50 when the Senior PGA Tour began and won one of only two events the Tour held in 1980: the Suntree Classic. In 2004, he was inducted into the World Golf Hall of Fame.

Sifford won only one Champions Tour event, but he did win the 1975 Senior PGA Championship and seven Grand Champions events. He also became a grandfather figure to Tiger Woods. "The pain, suffering and sacrifice experienced by Mr. Sifford in being a lonely pioneer for black golfers on the PGA TOUR will never be forgotten by me," said Woods. "His success and personal conduct will provide a blueprint and inspiration for myself and other aspiring black TOUR players."

Charlie Sifford

Became the first African American to play full time on the PGA TOUR in 1960

* * *

Turned professional: 1952

* * *

Last year competing: 2003

* * *

PGA TOUR victories: Two

* * *

Champions Tour victories: One

* * *

Inducted into the World Golf Hall of Fame in 2004

WORLD GOLF
HALL of FAME

Sifford was subjected to taunts and death threats, and at times even had to change clothes and sleep in his car because many motels and country clubs were for whites only. A proud man, he endured and changed the face of the game, becoming the first African-American to win an event: the 1967 Greater Hartford Open. He won again in 1969 at the Los Angeles Open and had a solid career. But he never received an invitation to The Masters.

Although he won the 1969 Los Angeles Open, Sifford never received an invitation to The Masters.

Sam Snead, who was known for his folksy wisdom, often said, "Keep close count of your nickels and dimes, stay away from whiskey, and never concede a putt."

Sam Snead

A legend of the first order, Sam Snead's career lasted for decades—a longevity that is legendary in and of itself. He won his first professional tournament in 1936, and his last in 1982, at age 70. In between, he won a total of 82 official PGA TOUR events, a record that no one could touch. Independent record keepers credit Snead with 135 worldwide victories, another mark that most likely will never be broken.

Snead was born in 1912 in the backwoods of western Virginia. The story of his youth is legendary, telling of a barefoot young boy learning to swing makeshift clubs carved from tree limbs. Even then, he was a natural. His swing, never tampered with by a teacher, was silky smooth and admired by many. "Watching Sam Snead practice hitting golf balls is like watching a fish practice swimming," said John Schlee, runner-up in the 1973 U.S. Open.

That raw talent made Snead the first long hitter of the modern era. Stories were legion about how far Snead could hit the ball, even in the days of hickory shafts. In his first tournament, he drove the first green, 350 yards away, after hitting his first two drives out of bounds. "In those days, we used to think long hitters couldn't play well," said fellow legend Byron Nelson. "Well, he stopped that myth."

After turning pro in 1934, Snead won his first event—the West Virginia Closed Pro—in 1936. The next year, his career blossomed. He won five tournaments in 1937 and eight in 1938. In his first seven years on the PGA TOUR, he won 28 tournaments, all by the age of 30. In 1942, Snead won his first major championship, the PGA Championship, when it was still conducted at match play. He beat Jim Turnesa 2 and 1 at Seaview Country Club in Atlantic City.

Four years later, he made the trip to the shrine of golf at St. Andrews for the British Open. To say he was underwhelmed is an understatement. "What abandoned course is this?" Snead asked the man seated next to him on the train as it pulled in next to the Old Course. He won the tournament in his only appearance—in those days American pros did not usually play in the British Open because the travel expenses were prohibitive. In fact, a player from the United States could win the tournament and still lose money.

Snead won the first of his three Masters titles in 1949, shooting 67-67 in the final two rounds to beat Lloyd Mangrum and Johnny Bulla by two shots. He won again in 1952 after entering the final round tied with Ben Hogan. Hogan shot an uncharacteristic 79 in the final round; Snead shot 72 and won by four shots over Jack Burke Jr. In 1954, Snead was the benefactor of more unintentional Hogan charity.

Snead won his first major championship in 1942 at the PGA Championship, beating Jim Turnesa in the match play final.

Snead putts to win the first of his three Masters titles in 1949, finishing with a pair of 67s in the final two rounds.

One of the great rivalries in golf was between Snead and Ben Hogan (white cap, foreground), pictured during a match at the Houston Country Club.

Snead entered the final round three shots behind Hogan, who shot a 75 on Sunday, allowing Snead to draw even and force a Monday playoff, which Snead won, 70-71.

Twice more Snead won the PGA Championship, in 1949 and 1951, both at match play. The only gap in his résumé is the U.S. Open, the major that eluded him. He was runner-up in the Open four times, and remained haunted by his 1939 U.S. Open experience at the Philadelphia Country Club.

Because there were no score-boards on the course in those days, Snead didn't know where he stood when he reached the 18th tee. He believed he needed a birdie to win when in reality, a par would have sealed the title. He pulled his tee shot into the left rough and made an unceremonious triple-bogey seven to lose the championship.

In 1947, on the final hole of a playoff against Lew Worsham, Snead missed a 30-inch putt to lose. Just two years later, his three-putt from the edge of the green on the 71st hole gave the Open to Cary Middlecoff. Snead then shot a final-round 76 in 1953 at Oakmont to lose to Hogan by six.

Snead's last major championship win came at age 39, but his career was by no means over. He won 19 more tournaments in his 40s. At 52, he became the oldest winner of a PGA TOUR event when he captured his eighth Greensboro Open in 1965, his final TOUR victory.

But Snead was not finished. Before the Champions Tour was born, Snead dominated the senior set. He won six Senior PGA Championships and five World Seniors titles. An inaugural member of the World Golf Hall of Fame, he played on eight Ryder Cup teams, captained three times,

Snead, known to golf fans as "Slammin' Sam," was never without his trademark straw hat.

Sam Snead

Owns the most victories in PGA TOUR history, nine ahead of Nicklaus

* * *

Won a record 17 times on the PGA TOUR after his 40th birthday

* * *

Turned professional: 1934

* * *

Last year competing: 1987

* * *

PGA TOUR victories: 82, including three Masters, three PGA Championships, and the British Open

* * *

Inducted into the World Golf Hall of Fame: 1974

WORLD GOLF
HALL
of
FAME

When the USGA outlawed the croquet style he used, Snead adopted a sidesaddle putting style, which he demonstrates here at the 1974 PGA Championship, an event he won three times.

and won four Vardon Trophies for low scoring average. At age 62, he finished third in the 1974 PGA Championship behind winner Lee Trevino and Jack Nicklaus. In the 1979 Quad Cities Classic, he became the oldest player to shoot his age in a PGA TOUR event, shooting 67 and 66. The next year, he became one of the six founding members of the Champions Tour. For four years Snead supported the fledgling Tour faithfully, playing in every event on the schedule. Although he didn't win an individual event, he won the 1982 Liberty Mutual Legends of Golf at age 70 with partner Don January.

He recounted his secret for longevity in his 1962 book, *The Education of a Golfer*: "Some of the things I didn't have to be taught as a rookie traveling pro were to keep close count of my nickels and dimes, stay away from whiskey, and never concede a putt." Snead ended his career by becoming one of the honorary starters at The Masters beginning in 1984. He died in 2002, four days before his 90th birthday.

Sam Snead once said of his renowned natural swing, "When I was young, I'd play and practice all day.... My hands bled. Nobody worked as hard at golf as I did."

Craig Stadler came onto the
Champions Tour with a vengeance in
2004, winning the JELD-WEN
Tradition and The First Tee Open.

Craig Stadler

At 30, Craig Stadler was a man with a retirement plan. The way the Walrus had it figured, he would play for 14 more years and be done with golf. Instead, at 51, the rumpled one became the king of the Champions Tour. He was Player of the Year in 2004 with five wins, including the JELD-WEN Tradition. He also had a dozen top three finishes in 21 events, led the Tour in earnings at $2,306,066, and secured the Byron Nelson Award for low scoring average: 69.30.

Those five victories included three consecutive wins: the JELD-WEN, The First Tee Open at Pebble Beach presented by Wal-Mart, and the SAS

Stadler hits out of Rae's Creek on his way to winning The Masters in 1982, his crowning achievement and one of 13 PGA TOUR victories.

Championship. "It's been very smooth, very fluid, very easy," Stadler said of his performance in 2004. "I think it's just one of those little periods that hopefully you go through more than once."

Stadler is funny, self-deprecating, irascible, and mellow—sometimes all in 10 minutes or less. The wine connoisseur and former Masters champ starts with one of those grumpy harrumphs and eases into a smile.

"I go out, I play, I'm having a good time, and I'm not paying attention to what I'm shooting," Stadler said of his method on the course. "Not that I don't care, but I'm not adding it up in my head. You can call it a zone, or whatever you want to call it. Things are going right, and you're just going out and playing. You're not trying to make it happen. You're not pressing. It doesn't get any better than that."

It certainly doesn't. Stadler had 13 wins on the PGA TOUR. His greatest triumph came at the 1982 Masters with a one-hole playoff victory over Dan Pohl. Stadler had shot a 5-under 67 to take the third-round lead. Pohl came storming out of the pack with his second straight 67 on Sunday to tie Stadler, who had shot a 1-over 73 in the final round. Stadler needed only to make par on the first playoff hole to win the title.

Craig Stadler

Champions Tour Player of the Year in 2004

* * *

Leading money-winner on the PGA TOUR in 1982 with four victories

* * *

Winner of the 1973 U.S. Amateur

* * *

Turned professional: 1975

* * *

PGA TOUR victories: 13, including one Masters

* * *

Champions Tour victories: Eight, including one Ford Senior Players Championship and one JELD-WEN Tradition

Right before he turned 50, Stadler hit a TOUR career slump. He missed the cut in five of his first eight PGA TOUR events and finished dead last after making the cut at The Masters. After that, Stadler just focused on playing out his PGA TOUR eligibility and turning 50 so he could play on the Champions Tour.

Voted by his peers as Player of the Year in 2004, Stadler was lauded by Champions Tour president Rick George for combining "his own brand of flair with considerable shotmaking."

What did he do when he got there? He made his first Champions Tour win a major, the 2003 Ford Senior Players Championship in Dearborn, blowing the field away with a closing 66—his first time since 1996. A week later, he closed with a 63 to win the B.C. Open on the PGA TOUR. With that, the often-grumpy golfer became the first player to win on the Champions Tour and PGA TOUR in back-to-back events, and only the second player to win on both tours in the same year. Raymond Floyd had done it in 1992 by winning the Doral-Ryder Open on the PGA TOUR in March, when he was

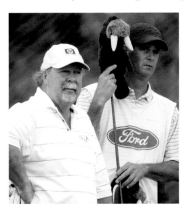

Defending champion Stadler, also known as "The Walrus," waits with his caddie on the second tee of the TPC of Michigan at the 2004 Ford Senior Players Championship.

still 49, and the GTE North Classic on the Champions Tour, just 16 days after turning 50.

"It's like la-la land here the last two weeks," Stadler said of his back-to-back victories. "I think the Ford Senior Players Championship meant a lot to me career-wise because you go out and look at all the wins I've had—and there haven't been that many—but it's probably the first time that I can remember I didn't have a three- or four-shot lead and someone folded," he said. "It's the first time I can remember just absolutely going out and winning a golf tournament."

Stadler's victory at the B.C. Open one week later was just as dynamic. He came from eight shots back in Endicott, with his youngest son, Chris, on his bag, shooting a 63 and beating Steve Lowery and Alex Cjeka by a shot.

"I was just kind of waiting until I turned 50 to see what would happen," he said. "And all of a sudden I learned how to play again. It's the magical number. Get a good bottle of wine, turn 50, and you start playing well."

Stadler won the Ford Senior Players Championship on the Champions Tour and the B.C. Open on the PGA TOUR in consecutive weeks during 2003.

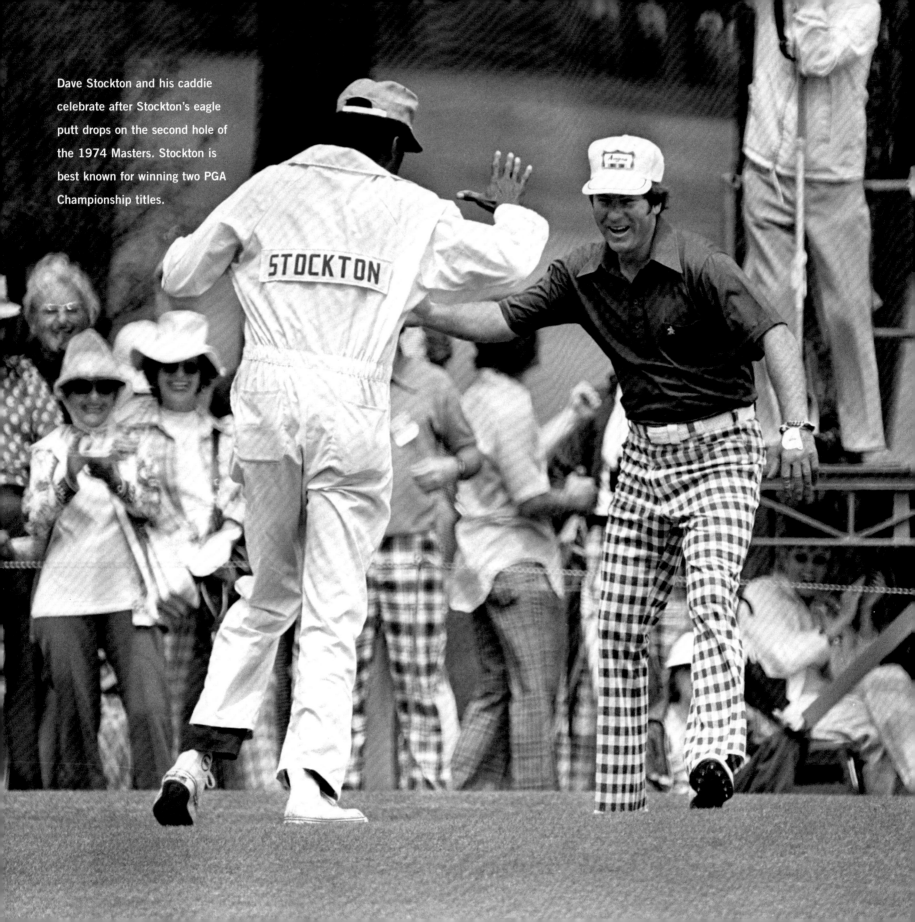

Dave Stockton and his caddie celebrate after Stockton's eagle putt drops on the second hole of the 1974 Masters. Stockton is best known for winning two PGA Championship titles.

Dave Stockton

The power of positive thinking seems to be embodied in Dave Stockton, a man whose swing wasn't always picture perfect, but whose tenacity was always textbook. Stockton is perhaps the least-known major championship winner, having taken two PGA Championship titles in the 1970s when players like Jack Nicklaus, Lee Trevino, and Tom Watson were in their prime and always in contention for the prize.

At the 1970 PGA Championship at Southern Hills, Stockton was as hot as the 100-degree-plus August sun. He shot two rounds of even par to share the lead at the halfway point, and then his putter got hot. Stockton shot a 4-under-par 66 that vaulted him to a three-shot lead. Nicklaus shot 66 on the final day, but it wasn't enough to catch Stockton, who bogeyed the final two holes but hung on for a two-stroke victory.

Stockton displayed all the grit he could muster at the 1976 PGA Championship at Congressional. Trailing by eight shots after 36 holes, Stockton shot 69 and cut the lead in half, trailing Charles Coody by four going into Sunday's final round. Stockton mounted a charge and took a two-shot lead over Don January with a birdie on the 11th hole. Then came Raymond Floyd, who birdied the 15th and 16th to join January one stroke behind Stockton. Coming to the final hole, Stockton needed a par to win. After a suspect drive, substandard second, and a pitch that left him 13 feet away, Stockton summoned all his strength and made the dramatic par putt to win the title.

Fifteen years later, he proved he was still solid by leading the Ryder Cup team to victory in 1991.

But while he made a good living on the PGA TOUR, corporate golf was always his priority; Stockton did more than

90 corporate events a year. "I was never committed to Dave Stockton's game," he said of his TOUR days. "I was committed to corporate America's golf game."

When he turned 50, he changed course and filled his schedule with Champions Tour events. He was named Rookie of the Year in 1992, winning five tournaments, and led the money list in 1993. In 1994 he led the money list again, winning three times.

Stockton always could putt. But when he turned 50, he found his tee-to-green game was stunning compared to the old days. Even Arnold Palmer asked him what he'd changed. Stockton said it was simple: "I started releasing my wrists and hitting draws."

In 1993, Stockton won a career-high five tournaments, the Arnold Palmer award, and led the Tour with $1,175,944. He followed that up with a $1,402,519 year in 1994. "I see myself now as a far more competitive player," he said then. "I think I'm one of the best. [Before] I conceded that role to guys like Raymond Floyd and Lee Trevino. Now, I don't consider myself inferior to anybody."

Dave Stockton

Topped the Champions Tour money list in 1993 and 1994

* * *

Turned professional: 1964

* * *

PGA TOUR victories: 10, including two PGA Championships

* * *

Champions Tour victories: 14, including two Ford Senior Players Championships and one U.S. Senior Open

Stockton raised his game a notch when he became a senior, adding an impressive long game to his already stellar putting.

Stockton's proudest moment came as captain of the 1991 Ryder Cup team when the Americans beat the Europeans in the "War by the Shore" at Kiawah Island, South Carolina.

Peter Thomson, who won the British
Open five times, accepts his fifth
Claret Jug at Royal Birkdale in 1965.

Peter Thomson

He is golf's Renaissance man. He is an accomplished player, a course architect, and a former broadcaster and writer. He was a Presidents Cup captain and a Commander of the Order of the British Empire. He even once ran for the Australian Parliament.

Perhaps most impressive, however, are Peter Thomson's five British Open titles. He still has his old Texas license plates, which read "5 TIMES." He is a member of the elite five-time British Open winners club along with Tom Watson, James Braid, and W. H. Taylor; only Harry Vardon won the

Thomson, who seemed to master all the difficult elements of the British Open, chips from the edge of a bunker on the way to his fourth British Open victory in 1958.

event six times. Thomson was the first man in the 1900s to win the event three times in a row. He also finished second three times.

Thomson loves fine wine and St. Andrews, where he and his wife spend the Australian winters. He's also a father of sorts to Australian golf—it is where he started his career and is primarily where he stayed. Yet despite his success in Australia and at the British Open, he never played the PGA TOUR full-time and won only once on the TOUR—the 1956 Texas International Open.

But when Thomson got the chance to play the Senior PGA Tour, he ran the tables. He and World Cup partner Kel Nagle made their debuts at the 1978 Liberty Mutual Legends of Golf tournament, scoring as runners-up to Gardner Dickinson and Sam Snead, but it was Thomson's pair of brilliant seasons in 1984 and 1985 that everyone remembers. Thomson won twice in 1984, including the Senior PGA Championship, and finished third on the money list.

An international star, Thomson shares a moment with the King, Arnold Palmer, before the Australian Open in 2004.

In 1985, he was flawless. He won nine times that year, starting his incredible season by beating Arnold Palmer and Billy Casper at The Vintage Invitational in March 1985, and concluding it in Melbourne, Florida, with a one-stroke win over Charlie Sifford.

He triggered his record run at The Vintage when he held off Palmer at the 18th hole. "Arnold hit an extraordinary shot from 200 yards out and it landed three feet from the hole," Thomson said. "I knew he was going to make three, so I had to par. I just nosed him out."

Thomson's 1985 season was reminiscent of Sam Snead's streak of 10 wins in 1950. Thomson, with daughter Peta Anne in tow, traveled from city to city, leading his events and pushing the previously dominant duo of Don January and Miller Barber—who had traded off

Peter Thomson

Won the British Open three years in a row (1954-1956)

* * *

Shares the Champions Tour record for most wins in a single year: Nine

* * *

Turned professional: 1949

* * *

Last year competing: 1990

* * *

PGA TOUR victories: Six, including five British Opens

* * *

Champions Tour victories: 11, including one Senior PGA Championship

* * *

Inducted into the World Golf Hall of Fame in 1988

WORLD GOLF
HALL
of
FAME

leading the money list for each of the first five years—to the side.

He had won the last two events he played in 1984, which gave him the confidence going into 1985. His daughter's bold prediction, that Thompson would win 10 times that year, also helped him sustain his fast start. "It became quite an extraordinary prediction," he said. "It was something we reflected on a lot."

Thomson almost won a 10th event, but wound up losing at the 18th hole to champion Harold Henning in the quarterfinals of the Seiko-Tucson Match Play. The following year, he was lining up a putt at the Doug Sanders Celebrity Classic in Houston when his eyesight blurred. "A cloud came over and my eyesight just went," Thomson said. "I went to contact lenses."

He lost that event by a shot to Bruce Crampton, but nothing was the same. "I was 56," Thomson said. "Old age had caught up with me." He returned to Australia at the end of the 1980s, where he continues to be active, designing courses around the world. He also captained the International team in The Presidents Cup three times, winning once when the event was played in Australia. He was elected into the World Golf Hall of Fame in 1988.

Thomson captained the International team at the 1996 Presidents Cup competition at Lake Manassas Golf Club in Virginia. He was also captain in 1998 and 2000.

Trevino smiled all the way to the
trophy presentation after he won
the British Open in 1972 at
Muirfield Golf Club in Scotland.

Lee Trevino

Tell Lee Trevino he can't say a word for 18 holes and he might not break 80. Or more likely, he would ignore you, tug on his pants, and whack a drive down the middle. Then he'd pick up his tee and start cackling and gesturing and talking to no one, yet everyone.

Everyone knows when Trevino is at an event. There's a crackle in the air, and the gallery is laughing a mile a minute—or roughly as fast as the Merry Mex is yapping. He talks even better than he plays, which is amazingly well for a kid from Dallas who hit balls with a Dr Pepper bottle and learned to hustle games at local courses before he could even drive a car.

Trevino needs about 15 seconds to concentrate on the shot at hand; once he's finished, he's slapping his thigh and talking nonstop. It's a wonder the kid from Texas stopped talking long enough to win 29 PGA TOUR events and an equal number on the Champions Tour.

He first caught everyone's attention at the 1967 U.S. Open when he finished fifth. The next year, he made a splash, winning the 1968 U.S. Open at Oak Hill Country Club. Not only did he win the national championship, he did so by beating golf's reigning heavyweight, Jack Nicklaus, by four shots.

Trevino's best year, though, was probably 1971. In June, he won the U.S. Open at Merion, where he beat Nicklaus by three shots in an 18-hole playoff. True to form, the Merry Mex pulled a rubber snake from his bag and tossed it at Nicklaus on

Trevino poses with a rubber snake he used to fling at Jack Nicklaus before their 1971 U.S. Open playoff, which Trevino won.

Always a deadly putter, Trevino drains one for a birdie on the way to his first PGA TOUR victory, the 1968 U.S. Open.

Trevino won six major championships, including the 1971 British Open at Royal Birkdale.

the first tee, before either had hit a shot. Nicklaus fell behind by two shots early in the playoff, and Trevino never gave an inch.

"I have no ambition to win all of the four major championships," Trevino said afterward. "I just want to win tournaments, whether it's the Screen Door Open or the Canadian Bacon Open. My ambition is to win a million dollars and when I do that I may go south of the border."

Actually, he did both—winning majors and a million dollars. The million would come later, but for a four-week stretch in 1971, Trevino was the best golfer in the world. During that span, he won the U.S. Open, the British Open, and the Canadian Open. He would win three more times that year, his best year as a professional.

In 1972, the British Open at Muirfield was billed as the Grand Slam Open because Nicklaus had won the Masters and U.S. Open that year. A victory at the British Open would give him leg three of the Slam. Nicklaus shot a final-round 66, but came up a shot short of Trevino.

Trevino won the PGA Championship in 1974 and 10 years later, added the sixth and final major of his career, winning his second PGA Championship at age 44. He won the Vardon Trophy for lowest scoring average five times, played on six Ryder Cup teams, and was elected into the World Golf Hall of Fame.

Trevino won the first of his four senior majors as a rookie when he shot 67 to beat Jack Nicklaus at the 1990 U.S. Senior Open. He went on to win two Senior PGA Championship titles in 1992 and 1994 and the 1992 JELD-WEN Tradition. And even when it looked as though Nicklaus might catch him in the closing holes at the 1990 U.S. Senior Open at Ridgewood Country Club, Trevino got the last word.

Sitting in the TV tower with a one-shot lead after having completed his final round, Trevino

---

Trevino pays homage to the club he loves best after sinking a putt at Shoal Creek to win the 1984 PGA Championship by four strokes.

Lee Trevino

Won the Vardon Trophy for lowest scoring average on the PGA TOUR a record five times

* * *

Turned professional: 1960

* * *

PGA TOUR victories: 29, including two U.S. Opens, two British Opens, and two PGA Championships

* * *

Champions Tour victories: 29, including two Senior PGA Championships, one U.S. Senior Open, and one JELD-WEN Tradition

* * *

Inducted into the World Golf Hall of Fame in 1981

WORLD GOLF
HALL
of
FAME

"Pressure is playing for ten dollars when you don't have a dime in your pocket." —LEE TREVINO

watched Nicklaus line up what looked to everyone else like a routine four-foot par putt at the 71st hole. If he made the putt, Nicklaus would have had a fighting chance to catch Trevino with a birdie at 18 and force a playoff.

Prophetically, Trevino, now shifting to television analyst, weighed in with an insider's insight: "Jack has a bad habit of looking up [and] if he looks up, he's going to lip it out on the right side." Sure enough, the putt promptly lipped out and the victorious Trevino screamed into the microphone, "Give me the trophy!"

Trevino's 1990 victory over Nicklaus brought him six wins for the year, and it was only

Trevino more than held his own against the legendary Jack Nicklaus. Of his game, Trevino said, "I'm not indebted to anyone for the game I've got. That's my single biggest source of satisfaction."

July 1. He had a letdown after that, but started fighting his way back with top 10 finishes. He came close at the Gatlin Brothers' Southwest Senior Classic in mid-October, finishing second to Bruce Crampton, then picked up his seventh title of the year at the Transamerica Senior Golf Championship, beating Mike Hill by two shots.

Trevino was the man of the year. In that magical 1990 season he had seven wins, eight seconds, and a scoring record of 68.69. He won Player and Rookie of the Year honors, became the first senior to win more than $1 million in a season ($1,190,518), and immediately took over first place on the all-time money list. He also won the most money of anyone on any tour that season, besting PGA TOUR leading money winner Greg Norman by $25,041. "It's like leading the league in batting average, runs batted in, and home runs," a pleased Trevino said. Two years later, he was number one again, this time with five wins in 1992—and still as gregarious and colorful as ever.

As a senior, Trevino came out of the gate charging, winning seven times in his rookie year on his way to a million-dollar season.

Tom Watson celebrates in the grand theater at Augusta National after sinking the winning putt at the 1977 Masters and earning the first of two green jackets.

Tom Watson

Tom Watson was center stage for two of the greatest tournaments of this generation. And both involved Jack Nicklaus. In 1977, at age 27—10 years younger than Nicklaus—Watson stared down the great man over 36 holes at Turnberry to win his second British Open title. Watson and Nicklaus were paired together for the final two days and each shot a 5-under-par 65 in the third round, putting them miles ahead of the pack. On the last day, the two played some of the best golf of the modern era. Nicklaus holed a 40-foot putt on the final hole for a 4-under-par 66.

That monster putt forced Watson to make a five-footer birdie to win, which he did with a 65. He also finished 11 shots in front of second runner-up Hubert Green, who, at 1-under 279, was the only other player to finish under par.

Watson stared down Nicklaus once again in April of that year, this time to win the 1977 Masters by shooting a final-round 67 and holding off a charging Nicklaus by two shots.

The two rivals also faced off at the 1982 U.S. Open at Pebble Beach. With nine holes to play in the championship, Watson and Nicklaus were tied. They stayed neck-in-neck until Watson came to the par-3 17th, a hole at which Nicklaus had hit the flagstick with a 1-iron to clinch the 1972 Open.

Watson pulled his tee shot left of the green, in the high rough with virtually no green to work with. As he surveyed the situation, his caddie, Bruce Edwards, told him to get it close. "I'm gonna

make it," Watson replied. The shot hit the flagstick and dropped into the hole for a birdie and a one-shot lead. He birdied the par-5 18th for a final margin of two strokes and the victory.

One of the greatest players ever, Watson owns five British Open titles, a record that's second only to Harry Vardon's six Claret Jugs. A member of the World Golf Hall of Fame, Watson won The Masters twice, along with his lone U.S. Open, for a total of eight major championships and 39 victories on the PGA TOUR. He was Player of the Year six times and won the Vardon Trophy for low scoring average three times.

As a senior, three of his six victories have been majors. But Watson has become as well known for his character as his golf skill. He spent the 2003 season promoting grace, courage, compassion, and commitment. He didn't set out to do that, but when his longtime caddie Bruce Edwards was diagnosed with an aggressive form of ALS, or Lou Gehrig's

Tom Watson

Ranks ninth on the all-time PGA TOUR victories list

* * *

Won at least three times each year from 1977 through 1982

* * *

Turned professional: 1971

* * *

PGA TOUR victories: 39, including five British Opens, two Masters, and one U.S. Open

* * *

Champions Tour victories: Six, including one Senior PGA Championship, one Senior British Open Championship, and one JELD-WEN Tradition

* * *

Inducted into the World Golf Hall of Fame in 1988

WORLD GOLF
HALL
of
FAME

Watson paired with old rival Jack Nicklaus in the 1981 Ryder Cup matches, which the United States won.

Watson's dramatic chip-in from high rough on the 17th at Pebble Beach propelled him to his U.S. Open victory in 1982 over Jack Nicklaus.

Able to get the ball up and down from anywhere, Watson hits from the sand on his way to winning the 1998 MasterCard Colonial, his 39th PGA TOUR victory.

Disease, Watson put the fight—for awareness and a cure—front and center. Watson's 2003 Player of the Year honors and career-best season on the Champions Tour will forever be an asterisk to what he did for Edwards and the fatal disease.

Edwards was too frail to make the trip to the Senior British Open that year, but Watson won it in his honor. Watson returned to Turnberry, the site of perhaps his greatest triumph, and shot a final-round 64, coupled with runner-up Carl Mason's double bogey, to force a playoff that Watson won with a par on the second hole.

A few weeks later, Watson and Edwards shared one last major title victory at the JELD-WEN Tradition. After shooting a 10-under-par 62 in the second round, Watson hung on to win with some 72nd hole dramatics. He got his ball up and down from a greenside bunker for a birdie and scored victory over Jim Ahern, Tom Kite, and Gil Morgan.

That same year, he also remarkably shared the lead at the U.S. Open after the first round.

Watson and longtime caddie Bruce Edwards were rarely apart for over 30 years of Watson's career.

Watson's close friend and caddie, Bruce Edwards, died of ALS the morning of the beginning of the 2004 Masters. Watson leads the fundraising fight for research to conquer the disease.

It was the fifth major on the two tours that year that Edwards was on the bag.

The JELD-WEN Tradition victory, however, stayed with him. "It was one of the things I wanted to do when Bruce was diagnosed," Watson said. "It was the only thing I wanted to do. I had a goal to win one more time with him on the bag."

Convictions have always come first for Watson. Whether it's politics, ALS, or social exclusion, Watson isn't shy. Within a week of Edwards's diagnosis, Watson had learned about every aspect of ALS he could. In 2003, he donated the $1 million annuity he earned for winning the Charles Schwab Cup to ALS research. He also teamed up with Edwards, former PGA TOUR player Jeff Julian—who also suffered from ALS—and the ALS Therapy Development Foundation to launch a fundraising campaign, Driving 4 Life.

Edwards lost his battle with ALS the morning of the first round of the 2004 Masters. Watson, however, continues the fight.

In 2003, Watson returned to Turnberry, the site of his 1977 British Open victory, to win at the Senior British Open in a playoff over Carl Mason (left).

THE WESTIN TURNBERRY RESORT

LEADER BOARD

HOLE	1	2	3	4	5	6	7	8	9	10	11	12	13	14	15	16	17	18	TOTAL
PAR	4	4	4	3	4	3	4	5	4	4	4	3	4	4	4	3	5	4	280
14 MASON C	14	14	14	15	15	15	16	16	17	17	18	18	18	18	18	18	19	17 ✦	263
13 WEIBRING	13	13	12	13	14	14	15	15	15	15	14	13	13	12	12	10	10		270
11 KITE	10	11	11	12	13	14	15	14	14	14	14	14	14	13	14	15	14		266
11 WATSON	12	12	12	13	13	13	13	14	16	16	16	16	16	16	17	18	17 ✦		263
11 SUMMERHAYS	10	10	10	11	11	12	13	13	13	12	12	13	13	13	14	15	16		264
10 COLBERT	9	9	9	10	10	10	11	10	10	9	9	8	8	8	6	6	7		273
9 McCUMBER	10	10	10	10	10	10	11	11	11	11	11	11	10	9	8	9	9		271
7 JONES	7	7	7	8	8	8	9	9	9	9	9	10	9	9	9	9			271
6 AOKI	6	6	7	8	7	6	6	6	6	6	7	6	6	6	6	6	5		275
6 ZOELLER	7	7	7	7	6	7	6	7	8	7	7	7	6	6	6	6	5		275
6 NICKLAUS	6	6	6	6	6	6	7	6	6	6	7	6	6	6	6	6	5		275
2 LONGMUIR	3	3	3	4	5	5	5	5	5	5	5	6	6	6	4	4	3		277
6 DURNIAN	6	7	7	7	7	8	8	9	10	11	10	10	9	8	8	8			272

The
TOUR

"I love the Champions Tour.
I played the same courses for 28 years,
and now I've got a new course every week....
It's awesome. I have a different attitude in
the first round. I come out firing."

—CRAIG STADLER

Jack Nicklaus, who now plays competitive golf sparingly, surprised himself—but not his fans or rivals—when he won the Senior Skins Game in 2005, earning the biggest check of his career.

Looking back now on the silver anniversary of the Champions Tour, it seems incedible that it all began at those first two Liberty Mutual Legends of Golf tournaments. Many fans remember those events as if they happened yesterday, yet it was way back in 1978 when Jimmy Demaret decided to hold a reunion for the 50-and-over set in Austin, Texas. Demaret set the date and then invited two dozen of his old friends from the fairways to grab their clubs, dust them off, and come down to Onion Creek Country Club for a little bit of golf.

Nothing about it was official. In fact, it didn't seem like much more than a chance to get out of the house and tell old stories. Today, we know better. What started as a gathering of long-time friends is now a significant part of the game, with 28 official tournaments and five major championships; a $1 million, season-long points race; and purses totaling more than $50 million. The average purse in 2005 was $1.8 million. Craig Stadler and Hale Irwin finished first and second on the 2004 money list, both with more than $2 million in earnings. Fourteen other players earned $1 million-plus.

But it's about more than just money. The Champions Tour is a place where Hale Irwin gets better with age. Where Arnold Palmer still reigns as King. Where Dana Quigley and Allen Doyle get another chance. Where Craig Stadler and Larry Nelson and Tom Watson kick their games into high gear rather than fade into what would have been retirement only 25 years ago.

Some Champions Tour players have won more in one year than they did in their entire careers on the PGA TOUR. Some have thrived in resurrecting their golf careers. Still others have been able to plan so they can spend their lives playing golf—from the PGA TOUR through retirement in their 60s or 70s. But it wasn't always that way.

Jimmy Demaret (left) and Sam Snead were two of the central figures at the Liberty Mutual Legends of Golf tournaments.

In the beginning, no one knew what would happen. Would the Legends of Golf be a nice little one- or two- or three-time event? Could the over-50 set be competitive? Would anyone want to watch them?

Demaret and promoter Fred Raphael wanted to find out. They threw their product in front of everyone, including PGA TOUR Commissioner Deane Beman and the TOUR Policy Board at a watershed meeting that turned out to set the Senior PGA Tour in motion.

Roberto De Vicenzo was part of the legendary playoff in the 1978 Liberty Mutual Legends of Golf competition. That action-packed playoff jump-started the idea of a tour for golfers over 50.

But the groundwork was formally laid at a meeting on January 16, 1980, when Beman met with Sam Snead, Bob Goalby, Julius Boros, Don January, Dan Sikes, and Gardner Dickinson. At that meeting, Sikes was named chairman of the advisory council and Snead the honorary chairman.

"It was part of a comprehensive program," said Beman, explaining the appeal of the new plan. "You've got to remember the times. Golf was on the downslide. Tennis was kicking us all over the place television-wise. It was a time of decline for golf. Bowling was bigger than golf." But not for long.

Five months later, the seniors were teeing it up in their first official event. January won that inaugural tournament—the $125,000 Atlantic City Senior International—beating Mike Souchak by two shots. Then in November, Charlie Sifford won the $125,000 Suntree Classic by four shots over January. In between, Roberto De Vicenzo won the U.S. Senior Open, and Arnold Palmer closed out the year by winning the Senior PGA Championship. Both were unofficial events at the time.

Those four events set the tone for 1981, when the Tour grew to seven events—five of them official—and an official total purse of $750,000. By July 1986, the seniors had celebrated their 100th event, the MONY Syracuse Seniors Pro Golf Classic, and there was no slowing them down.

The man behind the schedule expansion was Brian Henning, who had been commissioner of South Africa's golf tour, but immigrated to the United States in the late 1970s. Henning, known to

Don January, one of the six founders of the Senior PGA Tour, renamed the Champions Tour in 2002, dominated the early days of the Tour with his stellar play.

Charlie Sifford won the second event on the fledgling Senior PGA Tour, the Suntree Classic.

everyone as Bruno, was hired in 1981 as the Tour's tournament director, setting up events, and marketing and promoting the Tour. Henning would negotiate the contracts with the tournament organizers, then go in and teach them to run the events—everything from roping and staking to setting up tee times and pro-am parties. At the same time, he served as rules official, kept players apprised of the schedule, and helped set the rules for the fledgling Tour.

"Bruno was instrumental," Beman said. "He was the point guy. He was the guy who put it

Brian Henning, known as "Bruno" to the players, was a key figure in the early development and success of the Tour.

together, held it together, and nurtured it from day one."

Henning worked tirelessly to nurture the dreams of a few golfers. "Our goal was to get about 10 events, just to get them out of house for a few weeks each year—to get the boys together," Henning said. "Kind of like a nostalgia tour. . . . My job was to go find sponsors and Deane Beman gave me the green light and the pencil and just said, 'Go out and do the job. Whatever you can find.'"

Henning landed the first big event in 1983, the Senior Tournament Players Championship. But while purses began to creep upward, the Legends tournament—because of the format, the field, and the history—was the only televised senior event in the first few years. And it remained unofficial until 2002.

The first five years of the Tour seemed to be a private playground for Texas buddies Don January and Miller Barber. They combined for 25 victories, and one or the other led the money list from 1980 to 1984. The reason was obvious: both had played the PGA TOUR well into their 40s—January had won the Vardon Trophy for low scoring average in 1976 at age 46.

They set the stage for the Trevinos and Irwins to follow. January finished first, second, and third in 1980 in the only three events he played, and finished in the top three in five of the six events he played in 1981. Barber turned 50 in 1981 and proceeded to finish in the top 10 in every event that year and followed up with 24 top 10s in a combined 31 events in 1982 and 1983.

"Everyone else who took the field had had a sabbatical of anywhere from five to 15 years without any competition," January said. "A lot of them didn't even play golf. They were in other businesses. [Playing into your 40s] was a distinct advantage then."

But the seniors didn't just finish playing and head to their hotel. They were selling themselves and the Tour in the early years, so they went to every party thrown during the week—pro-am parties, draw parties, sponsor parties. Attendance was mandatory. "We always said, 'If you don't want to do this, you don't have to be out here,'" Barber said. "'This is an obligation.' So we all put on our coats and ties and went to the parties."

And they had fun.

"These guys were not only there to get away from the house, they were there to thank the people who allowed them that opportunity," Henning said. "Sometimes we had three and four parties a week. And when Sam Snead and Lionel

Hebert would come out with their trumpets, no telling what would happen."

Much of the early success can be attributed to Snead, Bolt, and Boros—the pioneer group's front men. "Without those three names, without those guys out front, we wouldn't have made it," Goalby remembered. "Especially Sam. He played every tournament for four years and went to every party, every banquet, and put on every clinic. Sam loved senior golf, he loved us, and he wanted to help. If Snead was in town, we needed him. And he never squawked." Goalby stayed active longer than anyone else, serving on the senior board for 16 years. And he was the one who pressed players who were, at times, reluctant to commit to the cause.

"Every one who joined to be a Senior Tour player committed to play in every tournament we scheduled," Beman said. "So when we went out to a community, we had a list of players—all of the members who had guaranteed their appearance. I wouldn't underestimate that. That was the first time it had ever been done by players—before or since."

That entertainment factor set the seniors apart. Designed to be a totally different product from the PGA TOUR, the Senior PGA Tour wasn't all competition, but rather a combination of competition and fan-friendly entertainment.

"We had the best players with the greatest names and greatest pedigrees in the history of golf, and they had a passion for the competition," Beman said. "So when we developed the eligibility and the pro-am formats, we developed a distinct product."

Sam Snead, one of the game's great legends, played in every Senior PGA Tour event in the first four years of the Tour.

Arnold Palmer's arrival on the scene was a godsend for the Tour, drawing larger crowds and increased interest in the tournaments.

It didn't hurt that the cast kept adding star power every few years. Snead and Boros helped carry the load until Palmer started to play, when more fans came out to support the King. Even Palmer's limited presence was enough to trigger more corporate involvement and get things rolling for the first television contract in 1985.

One of the more popular events the seniors added to the mix was Tuesday's Merrill Lynch Shootout, a fun nine-hole event where players were eliminated each hole. It kicked off each week in style. "It would all start on the first tee before I introduced the players," Henning said. "I'd let Arnold stand up to tee off, and just before he hit the ball I'd step in front of him and say, 'Arnold, what kind of ball are you playing?' I'd look at it, then I'd go give it to one of the spectators. He'd just look at me. And I'd take another one and do it. And another one. People loved it."

They got creative with weather problems, too. At the 1989 Bell Atlantic/St. Christopher's Classic, the pro-ams were rained out, so officials brought in sand and rubber ducks and built a par-3 inside the Valley Forge Convention Center. ESPN added audio, and disaster turned into a day of fun.

But nothing added more punch to the Tour than Palmer. When he turned 50 on September 10, 1979, the seniors had their first superstar. And although his busy off-course schedule kept him from playing too many events, when Palmer did play, he drew crowds, sponsors, and new fans.

To this day his involvement guarantees a tournament's success. Just as important, however, the Champions Tour has also allowed him another 25 years of competition in the game he loves.

Neither Palmer nor Nicklaus, who was 10 years younger, played enough to lead the Champions Tour money list, but just their presence— Nicklaus won eight senior majors— brought a huge star-power surge.

"They had Sam the first two years—he was kind of the ignition key," Watson said. "Then Arnold coming on board obviously sold the Tour—that was the rocket. When Trevino came on, it gave them a second booster rocket. And then Jack was the retro rocket; he kept things steady."

Trevino left behind a budding television career in 1990 and showed the older set what a rookie could do, winning five times. He and Chi Chi Rodriguez were perfect additions to the

Jack Nicklaus provided another shot in the arm for the Tour when he turned 50 and joined the circuit.

entertaining format—Rodriguez with his swordplay and dancing, Trevino with his gift of gab. Both of them were Technicolor players in fields of polite nostalgia, and they drew more fans than everyone, save Palmer.

Rodriguez won seven times in 1987 and became the first player to pass the half-million mark in a season. Three years later, Trevino hit the ground running and didn't slow down. He relinquished his 1990 money title to Mike Hill in 1991, but took it right back in 1992. Ironically, he and Hill teamed to win the Liberty Mutual Legends of Golf four times—1991, 1992, 1994, and 1995. And most of those years, they were both in the list of top five money winners.

By the early 1990s, many of the pioneers were either playing only ceremonially or had retired. In the early years of the Tour, a player's most productive years seemed to be 50 to 55—those first few years after their transition from the PGA TOUR. After that, they turned human again.

The Champions Tour soon became a place for second and third careers. Walt Zembriski, a former steel worker who played a bit on the PGA TOUR, won three events in the late 1980s and pocketed more than $3 million. Texas farmer Robert Landers, who taught himself to play on his farm, qualified for the Champions Tour in 1994 and became a player to watch. And in 1991 Jim Albus became the first club pro to win a senior major—what is now the Ford Senior Players Championship.

"It has been a whole new life for a lot of people," Palmer said. "It's like the rising for a lot of the guys who never quite made it. And now, here's an opportunity to become self-sufficient in their own right."

Dave Stockton had a solid PGA TOUR career, but his fortune skyrocketed when he won back-to-back money titles and a combined eight tournaments in 1993 and 1994. In his mid-50s, Jim Colbert followed up with money titles in 1995 and 1996.

Robert Landers, a farmer-turned-professional golfer, was one of the greatest human interest stories on the Champions Tour.

Mike Hill (left) and Lee Trevino were a formidable force at the 1996 Liberty Mutual Legends of Golf.

Hale Irwin dominated the Champions Tour during the 1990s and into the new millennium.

Hale Irwin ran the tables after that. It took him a year or so to settle into the senior circuit, but when he did, visions of Tiger Woods-caliber wins came to mind: 16 wins, two Player of the Year awards, a record-setting scoring average (68.59 in 1997), an incredible string of top five finishes, and $5.3 million in the bank. And that was just in Irwin's first two incredible seasons of 1997 and 1998.

By the end of 2004, Irwin had added another Player of the Year and money title (his first came in 2002), 20 more victories for a total of 40 Champions Tour victories, and two Charles Schwab Cups—the second coming in 2004 at age 59 when he won twice, finished second twice, and was second on the money list to Stadler.

Between 1998 and 2002, Irwin continued to finish in the top five on the money list, while Bruce Fleisher, Larry Nelson, and Allen Doyle all took turns winning the Charles Schwab Cup, the Tour's top honor. In 2003, it went to Tom Watson, who played the entire season while helping his longtime caddie, Bruce Edwards, fight a losing battle with ALS (Lou Gehrig's Disease).

In 2003, Craig Stadler became the first player to win on the Champions Tour and PGA TOUR in back-to-back weeks. After becoming the youngest player to win a Champions Tour major at the Ford Senior Players Championship, Stadler went to the B.C. Open the following week, where he beat Alex Cjeka and Steve Lowery by a shot. And he had never planned to play this far into his career.

"I remember when I was about 30, I'd set up a whole retirement plan that I was going to retire at 44 and be done with golf," chuckled Stadler, who won five times in 2004 and was Player of the Year. "So much for that."

Many of Stadler's predecessors have come and gone, but Palmer is still out there, continuing to pack the fans onto the fairways and transcend the game. For many of them, what was once a nostalgic lawn party has become the next stage in a career that began back in the 1970s. Or the professional golf career that players like Doyle and Quigley never had.

"All of a sudden, there's more money here than they've made in a lifetime," Ray Floyd said.

Today, players start thinking about the Champions Tour early. Amateurs, former major league pitchers, and businessmen start plotting a path to the Champions Tour Qualifying School when they're in their 40s.

One of the new stars of the Champions Tour, Craig Stadler still has the ability to win on the PGA TOUR.

Meanwhile, professionals such as Bruce Lietzke are among the first generation of PGA TOUR players who can spend their entire career playing golf and never look for a club job or a second career.

In 2003, the Champions Tour implemented new fan features, which included live interviews during play, honorary observers who were allowed to walk inside the ropes, behind-the-scenes tours, and caddies for a day. And, while it took some

Bruce Lietzke is one of a new breed of seniors who remained active on the PGA TOUR into their late 40s to bridge themselves to another career on the Champions Tour.

adjusting for the players to have TV analysts and fans talking to them during rounds, the interaction proved to be a hit with the fans.

"We have been trained not to allow distractions out there," Lietzke said. "I had to kind of retrain myself to lose focus a bit between shots. Once we're over the golf ball, it's still the game of golf. And we refocus. But there are more distractions. If someone wants to ask me something, even if I did just lose a one-shot lead on the last hole, I make myself go over there and talk about it. Because no other tour does that, I think that adds to our Tour."

Over the years, the seniors have lost some of the familiar faces—Boros, Snead, Dickinson, the Hebert brothers—while others like Beman, Goalby, and January are all too often out of sight and out of mind. But their legacy continues on.

"For all the things I've done in golf, including winning The Masters, finishing second in the Open and the PGA, winning 14 times, and having the all-time record in birdies, I guess I was more satisfied—inner satisfaction—with my role with the seniors than anything else I've done in golf," Goalby said.

"You never ever could have known this would happen," Quigley said. "And for those guys to watch it grow to where it is now, it must be a great privilege for them."

Just as it is a privilege for those millions of fans who have watched the careers of their favorites continue to grow.

The sense of camaraderie,
displayed here at the 2000 U.S.
Senior Open by Bruce Fleisher
(left) and Hale Irwin, is character-
istic of the Champions Tour.

25 MEMORABLE
MOMENTS

In the 25 years since the Champions Tour was founded, 762 events have been played. These tournaments have produced an incredible collection of moments in golf history. On its 25th anniversary in 2005, the Tour celebrates its most memorable moments, in chronological order, as selected by a panel of experts.

1979 Liberty Mutual Legends of Golf

In the second year of the event, a national audience on NBC witnesses Roberto De Vicenzo and Julius Boros outduel Tommy Bolt and Art Wall in a birdie-fest six-hole playoff. The dramatics give credibility to the idea that there is a market for senior professional golf, launching what is now the Champions Tour.

1980 Atlantic City Senior International

Don January, one of the founding members of the Champions Tour, wins the first official Champions Tour event, defeating Mike Souchak by two strokes.

1980 Senior PGA Championship

Arnold Palmer wins his first Champions Tour start on the first hole of a playoff and helps spur interest in the fledgling Tour, much as he had done for the PGA TOUR during the 1950s and 1960s.

1985 Barnett Suntree Senior Classic

Five-time British Open champion Peter Thomson wins his ninth tournament of the year to set a record that is only equaled by Hale Irwin 12 years later.

1987 Senior Players Reunion Pro-Am

Fan favorite Chi Chi Rodriguez wins his fourth tournament in a row to set a Champions Tour record that still stands.

1988 Crestar Classic

Here, Arnold Palmer's last official win, his 10th on the Champions Tour and the 72nd of his career, comes just a week after his 59th birthday.

1990 Senior PGA Championship

Paired with Jack Nicklaus and Lee Trevino, Gary Player wins his sixth and final Champions Tour major, finishing play in the dark.

1990 Doug Sanders Kingwood Celebrity Classic

President George H. W. Bush participates in the pro-am tournament, the first time a sitting U.S. president participates in a PGA TOUR-sanctioned event.

1990 Ford Senior Players Championship

Jack Nicklaus sets the Champions Tour all-time 72-hole scoring record with a 27-under-par 261 at the 1990 Ford Senior Players Championship—then called the Mazda Senior Tournament Players Championship.

1990 Transamerica
Lee Trevino wins his seventh title en route to being named Player of the Year and Rookie of the Year. He is the first to surpass $1 million in official earnings and is the leading money winner in all of golf.

1991 U.S. Senior Open
Chi Chi Rodriguez makes a spectacular birdie on the 72nd hole to force a playoff, but Jack Nicklaus wins the 18-hole playoff to complete his senior career grand slam.

1991 GTE Northwest Classic
Joe Jimenez becomes the youngest pro to better his age by shooting 63 at the age of 65 in the second round at the GTE Northwest.

1993 GTE North Classic
Ray Floyd wins on the Champions Tour just months after winning at Doral on the PGA TOUR, becoming the first player to win on both tours in same year.

1994 Franklin Quest Championship
Tom Weiskopf drains several long putts on the closing holes to beat Dave Stockton in a playoff—a fitting tribute to his friend Bert Yancey, who passed away the same week.

1996 The Tradition
Jack Nicklaus scores a double eagle on the way to his fourth Tradition title. It is his last Champions Tour title and his 100th professional win.

1997 Northville Long Island Classic
Dana Quigley wins his first Champions Tour title, only to learn afterward that his father had lost his battle with cancer earlier in the day.

1997 Emerald Coast Classic
Isao Aoki becomes the first Champions Tour player to shoot 60, and then defeats Gil Morgan in a playoff for the title.

1997 Career Achievement
During the 1997 season Hale Irwin wins nine tournaments, tying Peter Thomson's record, and is the first to win $2 million in a single season.

1999 Emerald Coast Classic
Bob Duval wins the Champions Tour title and then watches his son David win THE PLAYERS Championship later that same day—the first time a father-son team scores victories in the same year.

1999 Nationwide Championship
Hale Irwin holes a 74-yard wedge shot for an eagle on the final hole to win. He then recreates his infamous U.S. Open reaction by running around and high-fiving members of the gallery.

2001 Charles Schwab Cup Championship
Allen Doyle wins the first Charles Schwab Cup and donates the entire $1 million annuity to six charities.

2002 SBC Senior Classic
Tom Kite birdies the final hole after Tom Watson pitches in from 41 yards, and Gil Morgan just misses a tying double eagle. Kite then defeats Watson on the second hole of sudden death.

2002 U.S. Senior Open
Senior Open qualifier Don Pooley outlasts Tom Watson in an epic six-hole sudden-death playoff for his first Champions Tour win.

2003 Ford Senior Players Championship
Craig Stadler wins on the Champions Tour and wins again on the PGA TOUR the following week; Stadler is the first Champions Tour player to do this.

2003 JELD-WEN Tradition
Tom Watson wins with his longtime friend and caddie Bruce Edwards, who is battling ALS (Lou Gehrig's Disease); Edwards succumbs to ALS six months later.

Photo Credits

©2004 Historic Golf Photos: 34, 38, 46, 70, 84, 94, 100, 104, 108, 130, 133, 140, 167, 173

A. Jones/Evening Standard/Getty Images: 4-5

Adam Pretty/Getty Images: 151

Allan Grant/Time Life Pictures/Getty Images: 152

Andy Lyons/Getty Images: 63, 79, 81, 116, 126, 186, 187

AP/Wide World Photos: 37, 45, 50, 60, 71, 88, 118, 157

©Bettmann/CORBIS: 2-3, 18, 20, 26, 30, 36, 39, 40, 42, 49, 55, 59, 64, 76, 77, 92, 95, 96, 103, 105, 110, 111, 122, 129, 132, 135, 144, 150, 156, 159, 165, 180

Central Press/Getty Images: 32, 113

Chris Condon/PGATOUR via WireImg/WireImage.com: 23, 28

Chris McGrath/Getty Images: 54

Chris Smith/The Observer/Getty Images: 52

Craig Jones/Getty Images: 19, 143, 185

David Cannon/Getty Images: 147, 160, 169

Donald Uhrbrock/Time Life Pictures/Getty Images: 48, 134

Elsa Hasch/Getty Images: 74

Evening Standard/Getty Images: 125

Ezra Shaw/Getty Images: 67

Gary Newkirk/Getty Images: 107, 123, 175, 178

George Tiedemann/Sports Illustrated: 89

Getty Images: 21, 98, 114, 148, 154, 158, 161

Golf Magazine/Fred Vuich: 91, 176

Golf Magazine/Tony Roberts: 6-7

Harry How/Getty Images: 138

J.D. Cuban/Getty Images: 51, 72, 124, 128, 153, 182

Jacquelime Duvoisin/Sports Illustrated: 120

Jacques Demarthon/AFP/Getty Images: 174

Jamal Wilson/AFP/Getty Images: 112

James Drake/Sports Illustrated: 136

John M. Burgess/Time Life Pictures/Getty Images: 183

©John Sommers/Reuters/CORBIS: 99

Jonathan Ferrey/Getty Images: 29, 168

Kimberly Barth/AFP/Getty Images: 106

Leonard Kamsler: 43, 44, 58, 68, 78, 85, 86, 97, 102, 137

©Lynda Richardson/CORBIS: 179

Phil Inglis/Getty Images: 115

Robert Beck/Sports Illustrated: 166

Scott Halleran/Getty Images: 8-9, 22, 62, 66, 90, 119, 141, 142, 146, 172, 181

Stan Honda/AFP/Getty Images: 14

Stephen Dunn/Getty Images: 33

Tony Duffy/Getty Images: 164

©Tony Roberts/CORBIS: 56, 73, 82, 162

Zoran Milich/Getty Images: 80, 184

"Baseball players quit playing, and they take up golf.
Basketball players quit, take up golf.
Football players quit, take up golf.
What are we supposed to take up when we quit?"

—GEORGE ARCHER